STICKMAKING

A COMPLETE COURSE

STICKMAKING

A COMPLETE COURSE

ANDREW JONES AND CLIVE GEORGE

GUILD OF MASTER CRAFTSMAN PUBLICATIONS

First published 1998 by
Guild of Master Craftsman Publications Ltd,
166 High Street, Lewes,
East Sussex, BN7 1XU

© Andrew Jones and Clive George 1998

ISBN 1 86108 083 2

All photographs by Andrew Jones and Clive George except:
Image Photographic Specialists
photographs without Fig numbers, on pages v, 2, 21, 22, 23, 30, 33, 34, 43, 47, 51, 55, 61, 71, 80, 91, 92, 109, 113, 117, 118, 141, 142, 143, and 150; and Figs 2.1, 2.15, 4.4, 7.1, 8.16, 9.25, 10.5, 10.9, 10.11, 10.17, 10.22
Anthony Bailey
photograph on page 128
Brian Thomas
Fig 8.13
Ian James
Figs 9.1, 9.3, 9.4, 9.5, 9.6, 9.8, 9.9, 9.10, 9.11, 9.12, 9.13, and 9.14
Steve Kime
Fig 10.15 and photographs without Fig numbers on pages 135, 136 and 137

Line drawings by John Yates

Designed by Mind's Eye Design, Lewes.

Typeface: Goudy and Stone Sans

Colour reproduction by Job Color srl - Gorle (BG) - Italy
Printed in Hong Kong by Genius Productions Ltd

*This book is dedicated to the memory of
John Wynford George who, in the truest sense,
was a gentle man.*

Andrew Jones and some of his 'silver'.

*In 1989, when the Champion Stickmaker's Shield was offered for the
first time at the Welsh Game and Country Pursuits Fair, it was won
by Andrew's uncle Jim Jones, who died during the writing of this
book. It is a fitting tribute to him that, this year, in a competition
involving more than 300 sticks, Andrew won the same shield.*

ACKNOWLEDGEMENTS

We are grateful to the following master stickmakers who so generously provided us with examples of their work for inclusion in this book:

Bob Griff Jones
Ian James
Glyn Gillard
Brian Thomas
Steve Kime
Tony Reed
Paul Egan

We are especially grateful to Irena Fullard for typing the manuscript and for the helpful suggestions she made towards improving it.

MEASUREMENTS
Although care has been taken to ensure that metric equivalents are true and accurate, they are only conversions from imperial. Throughout the book, instances may be found where an imperial measurement has slightly varying metric equivalents. Care should be taken to use either imperial or metric measurements consistently.

CONTENTS

FOREWORD

In 1996, because of my declared interest in stickmaking, I was invited to become President of the Association of South Wales Stickmakers and, in that capacity, I am pleased to have been asked to contribute the foreword to this book.

My family background is in farming and I have long admired the people and the skills associated with this industry, which has one of its strongholds in Wales. Agriculture is an industry where traditional skills are still nurtured, none more so than in the craft of stickmaking.

Historically, stickmaking developed in those areas of Britain which had large populations of sheep – particularly the horned breeds which provided the necessary raw materials. But the popularity of this craft has since extended well beyond both geographical and industrial boundaries.

Today, stickmakers are to be found throughout the country and in all walks of life. Competitions abound and associations with enthusiastic devotees promote the craft and encourage new members.

This book is intended to assist that process and, in my academic capacity, I applaud its philosophy of 'learning by doing'. It introduces the techniques involved by building knowledge progressively, starting with the simplest of sticks and culminating in the shepherd's badge of office – a crook made from ram's horn.

If it motivates just one more person to take up this fascinating craft, its authors will consider it a success: I hope it proves to be so.

R. H. Williams

Professor R. H. Williams, FRS
Vice-Chancellor
University of Wales, Swansea

INTRODUCTION

As I sit here waiting for inspiration, whilst watching a buzzard drift lazily over our bottom fields, my mind is taken back to the first time I met Andrew Jones.

Shortly after moving to this part of Wales, my wife and I were roped in to help with the local produce show and sheep dog trials – she on the craft section, me on the vegetables. I had finished my allotted tasks so I wandered over to see how my wife was getting on. She was helping someone to unpack and display his entry of walking sticks and crooks, and what a display they made.

I was particularly smitten by a crook with a shank of wondrous golden wood topped off by a jet black handle made, I was to discover, from buffalo horn. I asked the owner if he ever sold his sticks and we started a conversation which continued, with periods of interruption, for over two years and eventually resulted in my acquiring this stick of sticks from Andrew Jones.

From that first meeting our friendship developed, and with it came a suggestion from Andrew that we might together produce a book on stickmaking. A book which would explain, by thoroughly describing a number of progressive projects, the techniques involved in this craft. What follows is our attempt to do that.

Whilst this book is designed to impart knowledge in a structured way – each chapter building on the previous one – it also allows anyone with a more selective interest to proceed immediately with a particular project.

I sincerely hope that this book and the examples it contains will stimulate you to become involved with the craft of stickmaking and that you will derive as much pleasure from it as I have done over the years.

C. W. George
Pantmeddyg

Andrew and one of his specialities – the one-piece Cardigan stick –
at different stages of completion.

CHAPTER ONE

FINDING, CUTTING AND SEASONING STICKS

THE most difficult part of making a stick of any quality is finding good material to work with. As the craft of stickmaking increases in popularity, supplies of suitable ram's horn and deer antlers are less easy to acquire – certainly at reasonable cost – than even five years ago.

Fortunately, because wood is a renewable resource, it is still possible to obtain sufficient supplies to satisfy the needs of most stickmakers without causing conservation problems. Whilst it is increasingly possible to purchase (or beg) sticks which have been found and cut by someone else, for me that takes a lot of the enjoyment out of stickmaking, and finding the stick in the first place is good exercise too.

I live in a part of Wales which is not only one of the most beautiful but, because it is in the agricultural heartlands, is also one of the best places to find good wood from which to fashion sticks. The surrounding countryside is full of woodlands, mountains, rivers and streams – ideal locations and conditions for the trees and bushes which provide much of our raw material, at little or no cost. Whenever I'm moving sheep from one field to another or mending fences, I'm always on the lookout for something that will make a thumbstick, shank or interesting handle, and I rarely come home without having cut, or marked for later cutting, a stick or two.

A nose-in market stick. Holly shank topped with ram's horn handle.

WOODS USED IN STICKMAKING

What type of wood makes a good stick? It is true that you can make a perfectly acceptable stick from the wood of most trees: indeed, I have a Victorian stick manufacturer's catalogue which lists the availability of dozens of different sticks made from woods as exotic as ebony, aucuba, orange and olive. Whilst the choice of woods available in most countries today is more limited, it still offers an interesting range with which to work. Those that follow are generally available and I have used all of them at one time or another.

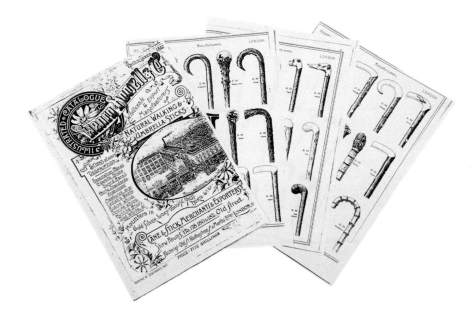

Fig 1.1 *Pages from a Victorian stick manufacturer's catalogue.*

ASH

A strong wood, resistant to splitting, the bark of which is a rather uninteresting grey. With care the outer bark can be buffed down to reveal a more colourful underbark.

Fig 1.2 *Ash tree saplings.*

BIRCH

Most people are familiar with the white bark of the silver birch, but young trees are deceptively brown. The wood itself is pale brown and even-grained, producing light yet strong sticks. With the bark left on, or peeled and stained, such sticks are very attractive.

Fig 1.3 Young silver birch is deceptively 'brown'.

BLACKTHORN

Felt by some to be the ultimate wood from which to produce sticks, there is no doubt that the best examples are very beautiful. However, such examples are very difficult to find and the wood is dense, which makes the stick heavy. The bush itself is extremely thorny, difficult, and sometimes downright dangerous to cut. Said to be the tree which provided Christ's crown-of-thorns, it has, over the centuries, been invested with all sorts of mystical powers. Branches, suckers or saplings of sufficient length and appropriate diameter are hard to come by and the degree of taper in a stick, particularly a long one, may be excessive (*see* page 9). If you find a good one, then rejoice. With its thorns trimmed back (not too much or you'll spoil the effect) and its rich bark varnished to a deep red hue, it will look magnificent.

CHESTNUT

The wood of the sweet chestnut provides those easily recognizable walking sticks available in outdoor pursuits shops and hospital out-patient departments. It is also used to fashion what is sold as a rather cumbersome 'shepherd's crook', although I cannot imagine many shepherds actually using one of these products! Nonetheless, chestnut *is* used to make large numbers of sticks which are cheap and functional. The bark is usually peeled and the wood coloured by staining, fuming or scorching (*see* Chapter 3, page 29).

HAWTHORN

Commonly found as a small hedgerow tree, and still planted to make stockproof hedges, hawthorn does not have the same character as blackthorn. Nevertheless, it does make good sticks though they are on the heavy side. The bark is drab, like chestnut, so it is usually peeled and the wood stained or fumed although, with care, the underbark may be retained to provide a pleasing effect.

HAZEL

This is a beautiful wood to work with. The tree, easily recognized by its catkins in the spring and its nuts in the autumn, throws up numerous shoots from its base, many of which are straight for the greater part of their length. This considerably reduces the amount of work required later to straighten the stick. The range of colours and effects in the bark, too, are many and varied – from a very dark brown to almost silver; from something like snakeskin to a lovely bird's-eye mottling. The wood seasons well, producing a strong stick, and it is easily obtainable.

Fig 1.4 *Hawthorn bushes are often planted as hedges.*

Fig 1.5 *A hazel tree with typical, numerous offshoots.*

HOLLY

The most instantly recognizable wood in this list, holly is better associated with Christmas decorations than with producing walking sticks. It is particularly difficult to season with the bark left on, as it inevitably wrinkles, and the effect is unacceptable. The wood itself is usually like ivory, and, when the bark is stripped, can be left in its natural state or coloured. Figure 1.7 shows a fine example of a holly stick with the Lord's Prayer engraved in a spiral along its length.

HONEYSUCKLE

I mention this plant not because it offers suitable wood itself, but because its climbing habit, and the effect this has on other trees, occasionally provides interesting material for the stickmaker. It has a tendency to twine itself around young saplings and, as they grow, the constricting effect of the honeysuckle produces a spiral which, in appearance, is not dissimilar to that of a corkscrew (*see* Fig 1.8). Such shanks, known as 'twisties', are highly prized by stickmakers.

Fig 1.6 *Hazel wood comes in a wide range of colours.*

Fig 1.7 *An engraved stick, made from holly.*

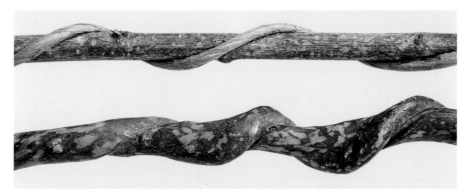

Fig 1.8 *An example of the corkscrew effect produced by twining honeysuckle.*

ROWAN (MOUNTAIN ASH)

The red berries of the rowan tree distinguish it and help identify saplings which might be good prospects from a distance! A tough, springy wood on the heavy side, it produces durable sticks of usable shapes and sizes.

SYCAMORE

This is so common now it has almost become a 'weed tree', and I am constantly removing seedlings which have taken root in our flower borders. Whilst younger trees produce branches which are straight and of sufficient length, the taper over such a length is very often excessive. This is a good wood to practise on, but not to spend too much time perfecting. There are better woods around.

WILLOW

Much the same can be said of this wood which is generally in plentiful supply, especially in wet ground. It produces straight shafts of good length, but the bark and the wood are characterless and cut sticks are 'whippy'. In a world which seems to contain an increasing number of disposable items, willow is the equivalent where sticks are concerned.

Fig 1.9 *A rowan tree – the distinctive red berries have started to dry.*

Fig 1.10 *The ubiquitous sycamore . . .*

Fig 1.11 *. . . and its distinctive leaves.*

Fig 1.12 *Though willows are plentiful, they do not produce good-quality sticks.*

FINDING WOOD

I'm often asked where I find my sticks and the answer I always give is, 'wherever I look for them'. If this sounds trite, that is not my intention, but there is no general rule that one can apply. Different woods grow in differing conditions and I can only repeat that whenever I'm out walking or working, I keep my eyes open for likely materials. I have found some excellent shanks, particularly of hawthorn and blackthorn, growing in hedgerows which have been laid (*see* Fig 1.13). Hedges which have been cut by a tractor-mounted flail rarely produce anything of value.

Any tree – particularly ash, sycamore and willow – which has been cut back close to ground level will usually generate new growth around its base and this can provide useful material (*see* Fig 1.14). Conversely, I have found that large mature trees, like ash, sycamore and chestnut, generally do not provide suitable shanks. If they do, they are usually too difficult to reach without a ladder and a good head for heights.

Some of the best hazel I have found has come from trees growing out of the banks of streams with their roots close to, or below, the water level. It seems to be that hazel growing on rough, stony ground produces more attractively patterned bark than that which grows in more fertile soil. As for birch, sycamore, ash, and rowan, they all produce saplings which not only make good shanks, but, when carefully dug up, provide a ready-made and very strong handle from the root (*see* Fig 1.15).

Whilst there may be no general rule about where to find suitable sticks, there *is* a more specific answer to the question 'When should I cut them?'. The old country saying is that you should always cut a stick whenever you see it because if you don't, someone else will! This salutary advice apart, the best time to cut sticks is during the winter months when the sap in the tree is not rising. So, aim for November, December or January. If you have to cut at other times, you need to be very careful with the seasoning process – more about that later (*see* page 11).

As to the size of sticks you're looking for, this will be determined by their intended purpose. A crook or a thumbstick will need to be longer, for example, than a conventional walking stick. A stick intended for a man may be heavier and larger in all of its dimensions than one for a woman or a young person.

A good length to aim for is between 4 and 5ft (1.2 and 1.5m), but I guarantee you will find a use for shanks either side of these dimensions so a broader, acceptable range is somewhere between 3 and 6ft (0.9 and 1.8m).

As for diameter, anything from ³⁄₄–1¹⁄₈in (19–29mm) is acceptable, the ideal being around 1in (25mm).

The balance of a finished stick is important and this can be critically affected by the extent to which a stick tapers over its length. Anything that tapers to half its diameter over its finished length is likely to be poorly balanced. Remember that the diameter of a stick shrinks a little during the drying process, and if the wood you are cutting is for a stick you propose to debark, that must also be taken into account. Although shrinkage is not a great problem, the knowledge that it occurs may help you to reject sticks which are already of borderline dimensions, whilst they are still on the tree.

Fig 1.13 *Hedgerows are a good source of shanks for sticks.*

Fig 1.14 *New growth from the base of trees that have been cut back can provide useful material.*

Fig 1.15 *A ready-made handle: the roots of birch, sycamore, ash and rowan can provide these.*

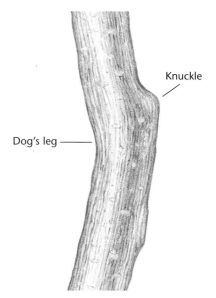

Fig 1.16 *Dog's legs and knuckles cannot be straightened.*

Do not be deterred by sticks which have bends in them; in most cases these can easily be removed after seasoning. The exception to this is a stick which has a 'knuckle' or a 'dog leg' in it (*see* Fig 1.16). Such bends cannot be removed satisfactorily: unless you can cut the stick above the knuckle, leave it. Better to look for another one.

If you are looking for potential thumbsticks, an important feature is the suitability of its 'vee' to accommodate the thumb comfortably. Whilst it is possible to make modest corrections to the depth of the vee by shaving off a little wood, ideally this should not be necessary. If the vee is too wide or too narrow it is possible to improve it (*see* Chapter 2, page 14). When cutting thumbsticks, do not cut the vee close to its finished length – which will be 2½–3in (640–760mm) – but leave it an inch (25mm) or so longer in case splits develop during seasoning.

Developing an eye for a good stick takes practice, but it will come. Although the first sticks you cut may not, when critically considered at home, match up to all these criteria, you will find something that will do to make a start. But not yet!

CUTTING WOOD

Having identified what it is we're looking for and where to find it, the next step should be to address the question, 'When I find it, how do I cut it?' I cut my first stick with a pocket knife. Whilst that same knife is still part of my kit, I have since acquired a few more tools which not only make the task a lot easier, but also reduce the risk of splitting or tearing the stick during the process of removal. You can see from Fig 1.17 that my kit for cutting sticks contains:

- a pocket knife (ideally this should have a means of locking the blade for safety);
- a folding saw of the type sold in most garden centres and tool shops as a 'pruning saw';
- a pair of secateurs for trimming off thorns and side shoots;
- a pair of old leather gloves and a pair of safety goggles (essential if you're taking on blackthorn or hawthorn);
- several lengths of baler twine (to tie up the sticks you cut, making them much easier to transport: any strong cord will do); and
- a trowel (useful for exposing roots prior to cutting them).

Pack these items into an old rucksack together with a meal for the day and you're off!

Before you cut so much as a twig, remember it probably *belongs* to someone. I know that I would object to finding someone on my land cutting sticks without my permission, so the first rule, unless you are on

Fig 1.17 *My basic stick cutting kit.*

common land, is to seek and obtain permission to be there for the
purpose of cutting sticks. The second rule is to tidy up when you've
finished. Don't just leave a pile of twigs or side shoots lying about, put
them back from whence they came. Otherwise, don't expect to be
welcomed back a second time!

SEASONING AND STORING WOOD

Having cut some suitable sticks, trimmed off any side shoots (not right
back to the base at this stage), bundled them carefully and got them
safely home, they must be seasoned. A typical 1in (25mm) thick shank
cut during the winter will need to be left to season for about 12 months.
One which has been cut at any other time of the year will need at least
another three months, and even then there is a chance that the cut ends
of the stick will split. A shank which has been cut with a section of
branch or root attached (from which a handle can be formed) may,
according to the size of the block, need up to two years to season properly.
To reduce the risk of splits, the ends of the block should be sealed with a
couple of coats of clear varnish or knotting liquid.

Before you tie up sticks for storing, give them a coat of woodworm oil, then tie them, top and bottom, in bundles of five or six and put them in an airy shed (an open-sided lean-to is ideal; a heated workshop is too warm). Stickmakers are divided as to whether bundles should be laid on the ground or stacked vertically: best of all, I believe, is to suspend the bundles from roof beams. This lets the air get to them, avoids any risk of bending and prevents any ground damp from affecting them (*see* Fig 1.18).

Rather like home-made wine, there is the temptation to try the product before it is ready. DON'T! If you start to work too soon, you will risk ruining all that you have achieved so far. Instead, be content that you have now stored in your shed a sufficient supply of material to see you through next year's winter months.

A year has gone by and the day for you to untie your sticks and start some serious stickmaking arrives. Take another good look at your collection and if you are in any way dissatisfied with one, discard it or give it to someone else. Don't waste your time trying to make a good stick out of a bad one – life's too short!

Fig 1.18 *A bundle of sticks suspended for seasoning.*

CHAPTER TWO

THUMBSTICKS

A THUMBSTICK is, in my opinion, one of the most comfortable and useful sticks it is possible to own. Not only does it serve as an aid to walking, the ultimate test of any good stick, but it also doubles as a rest for fishing rod, telescope or gun, as a means of deflecting troublesome brambles or branches on stick-hunting expeditions, and as a convenient tool for extricating wellie boots which have been sucked into bogs or river banks!

Relatively easy to produce, this is a good introduction to the craft of stickmaking since it incorporates three manufacturing processes common to the production of most sticks. It will certainly be good practice for the projects which follow. The three processes in question are:

1 straightening the shank (or shaft) of a stick;
2 fitting a ferrule; and
3 applying a varnish finish.

Varnished blackthorn thumbstick.

PROJECT

A NATURAL THUMBSTICK

A natural thumbstick can be found in any of the trees described in Chapter 1, but the best ones are likely to come from hazel or blackthorn. For this project I have chosen blackthorn.

SELECTING A STICK

Our first consideration in selecting one of the sticks from the bundle which has been seasoning for the past year is length. No matter what its other qualities might be, if a stick is not long enough to make a thumbstick it should be passed over. Because we are talking about blackthorn it can almost certainly be used to make something else.

What then is an appropriate length for a thumbstick? Given that people's height varies and the taller the person, the longer the stick should be, is there a way to determine the correct length? Yes, there is. At the beginning of this chapter I listed a variety of uses to which a thumbstick can be put. One I didn't mention is that it should provide a convenient crutch for its owner to lean on at the mart or in the pub when discussing the day's market prices! The best way to determine the length for a custom-made stick, therefore, is to take the measurement from the armpit (of the person for whom the stick is intended) to the ground. A thumbstick cut to that length will be comfortable to use: it will be in the range of 50–55in (1,300–1,400mm).

THE 'VEE'

Let's now move on to look at the suitability of the 'vee' in the stick you have selected. I should say immediately that faults in this particular area are many and varied. Some faults can be satisfactorily removed, others can be reduced. For example, if the vee is too narrow to take the thumb comfortably, it is perfectly acceptable to widen it by shaving its base (*see* Fig 2.2).

Fig 2.1 *A thumbstick should be comfortable to lean on.*

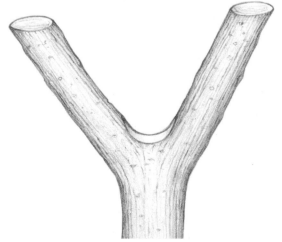

Fig 2.2 *Shaving the base of the vee to make it wider.*

Fig 2.3 *Squeezing a vee to reduce its width.*

Fig 2.4 *Trimming extra growths from a vee.*

Alternatively, it is possible to widen the vee slightly by heating it gently with a hot air gun (of the type used to strip paint), opening the vee a little, and inserting a wedge to keep it open while it cools. Be *very* careful not to split the stick down its length when carrying out this operation. Using the same technique, a vee which is too wide can be heated, squeezed in a vice with a wedge of the correct width in place, and held in this position with strong elastic bands (*see* Fig 2.3). Both of these operations should be undertaken *before* the sides of the vee have been trimmed to size. The longer the sides are, the easier it is to make any adjustments.

Some vees have additional shoots growing out from their base (*see* Fig 2.4). In most cases these can be carefully trimmed back so that they do not interfere with the proper shape of the vee.

You will be fortunate if the blackthorn you have selected has a perfect vee, so settle for what you've got. Improve it if you think you can, but always remember that you are dealing with a product of nature and not something which has come out of a factory mould. Blemishes, if that's what they are, help to give a stick its identity and character – never more so than in the case of blackthorn.

The sides of the vee should now be trimmed to size. They should be of equal length, between 2½–3in (640–760mm) long. The edges of the cut ends should then be finished. I do this by lightly sandpapering, taking care not to damage the bark. Another option, which I do not favour, is to round over the cut ends, taking off a little of the bark in the process. (*See* Fig 2.5.) This is very much a question of personal taste. I (and most other stickmakers it seems) prefer to see a clean, straight cut to the prongs of the vee, but ends rounded over are not a fault and would not be judged as such in a competition. If they are rounded off, a minimum of bark should be removed in the process – too much will make them look wrong.

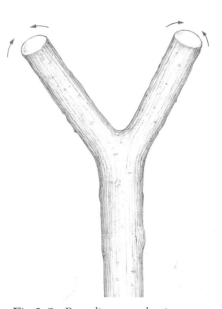

Fig 2.5 *Rounding over the tips.*

REMOVING BARK

Talking of the bark, it is now time to decide whether to leave the bark on your stick or to strip it off. For most stickmakers the very thought of removing the bark from a blackthorn is criminal. It is true that the bark when varnished is particularly attractive, but stickmakers should never be afraid to experiment. I have taken the bark off blackthorns (albeit ones which were not of the highest quality) with good effect. The knots which are left when the thorns have been cut back remain in evidence and if the shank is coloured, especially by the process of fuming, the results can be very attractive.

For this project we will assume that the chosen stick is of sufficient quality to justify leaving the bark on. The first step, therefore, is to tidy it up by carefully trimming the thorns and any side shoots right back to their base. This is best accomplished by using a pair of secateurs to trim them, and finishing them off with a small file. (*See* Figs 2.6 and 2.7.) Remember, do not take too much off the knots that are left from removal of the thorns. The quality of a blackthorn is determined by the frequency and symmetry of these knots so they must be left nicely rounded and *not* filed flat! (*See* Fig 2.8.)

Fig 2.6 *Trimming thorns and side shoots from the stick.*

Fig 2.7 *Smoothing down the knots left after trimming.*

Fig 2.8 *Do not file the knots flat – they should be left nicely rounded.*

STRAIGHTENING THE STICK

The next step is to straighten out any bends. To do this you need to apply some heat. There are two options: dry heat (produced by a hot air gun); or wet heat (i.e. steam). I prefer, and *always* use the steam method. Whilst it is difficult to damage the surface of a stick by over-exposure to steam, it is very easy to damage a stick irretrievably by giving it too much dry heat. However, the hot air gun comes into its own when bending other materials, which we shall look at later in this book (*see* Chapter 6, page 65).

Fig 2.9 *The steam from a kettle is sufficient to heat a single stick.*

Fig 2.10 *For heating a number of sticks, a water boiler is ideal. A draped coat will concentrate the heat where you want it.*

For a single stick, a kettle on a gas or electric ring is perfectly adequate (*see* Fig 2.9). For heating three or four at a time I find an old-fashioned water boiler powered by electricity to be absolutely ideal (*see* Fig 2.10). The old coat you can see in the photograph helps to concentrate the steam on the section of the stick where it's needed. A piece of sacking is similarly effective.

Work on each bend in turn. Expose it to the steam carefully for around 15 minutes and then, very gently, flex it over your leg until you feel it giving way and the bend starts to straighten (*see* Fig 2.11). Then, look at it again and, if satisfied, tackle the next bend. If it needs a little more straightening, try it over your leg again. If it doesn't move, put it back in to steam. You will be surprised at how easy it is to take bends out with this method. It is also a very satisfying process and I commend it to you. Once you have taken all of the bends out, lay the stick on a bench or table for a couple of hours to set.

Fig 2.11 *Flex the heated stick gently over your knee to straighten it.*

SAFE HEATING PRACTICES

A hot air gun is a very useful tool in stickmaking and we shall return to its applications in later chapters. This tool, by definition, generates considerable heat which is imparted to the stick and whilst it may be stating the obvious, extreme care is needed when handling wood which has been subjected to this or any other heating process.

It is important here to underline the need to follow safe practices when generating and working with steam. Without care it can lead to burns or, when contained, to explosions. For this reason, I do not favour the use of steamboxes as a method of heating sticks. They are not necessary and there are safer ways to achieve the same effect.

To avoid the risk of burns, *never* work close to steam without ensuring that your skin is properly protected. I strongly advise wearing industrial safety gloves when removing sticks from, or replacing them over, whatever means you are using to generate steam.

CUTTING TO SIZE

Next, decide on the length of stick you want. Remember the old carpenter's maxim: measure it twice and cut it once. For this job I clamp the stick in a vice, having first protected the bark by slipping a 3in (76mm) length of 1in (25mm) diameter plastic pipe, split in two lengthways, around the appropriate section. Providing the bark is protected, any suitable means of holding it steady will do. I use a hacksaw rather than a tenon saw because it produces a finer cut and reduces the risk of tearing the bark, but any fine-toothed saw should suit the purpose.

FITTING A FERRULE

The next step is to select and fit a ferrule to protect the bottom end of the stick before putting the finishing touches to it.

There are three choices of material for the ferrule: metal, rubber or horn. I shall deal with horn later (in Chapter 8) because, to my mind, such a ferrule goes best with a handle to match. As for rubber, whilst giving a good grip and being easy to fit (and replace) it always appears cumbersome to me. So, I am going to concentrate here on metal ferrules.

At its cheapest, a sawn-off piece of copper tubing will suffice, but it always looks just what it is. For the modest cost involved, a purpose-made, closed-ended ferrule in dull brass is the answer, being both neat and durable. Brass ferrules are available in a variety of sizes, ranging from ³⁄₈–1in (10–25mm), and can be purchased singly at game fairs and larger agricultural shows, or in quantities from the supplier listed on page 145.

To select one, measure the diameter of the stick an inch (25mm) or so in from its end. This will give you the size ferrule you need. Then, carefully cut through the bark around the circumference of the stick at a

Fig 2.12 *A collection of brass ferrules.*

Fig 2.13 *Cutting through the bark to fit a ferrule.*

point near the end which is *slightly* less than the length of the ferrule itself (*see* Fig 2.13). I use a junior hacksaw to make this cut; others prefer a sharp knife. The mark has three functions:

1 it serves as a working guide;
2 it prevents the bark above it from flaking off; and
3 it becomes the collar against which the ferrule will eventually sit.

Until you gain more practice and confidence, I recommend you stick a single turn of masking (or insulating) tape immediately above your mark in order to protect the bark from the next step, which is to rasp the end into a gentle taper to fit the ferrule (*see* Fig 2.14). The only problem with adhesive tape (whatever the type) is that it can be too sticky. On removal, it can tear off the bark which it was intended to protect. To minimize this risk, before putting it in place, press the strip you are going to apply onto another surface first – a dusty trouser leg is ideal! This will remove some, but not all of its adhesion and make it less likely to damage the bark on your stick. Try the ferrule for fit and, when it can be readily pushed on for about three-quarters of its length, remove it.

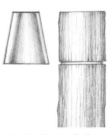

1 Cut through the bark round the circumference of the stick.

Tape

2 Rasp the end into a gentle taper.

3 Try the ferrule for fit.

4 Fix with a small veneer pin.

Fig 2.14 *Fitting a ferrule.*

At this stage many stickmakers tap the ferrule home and call it a day, but we will not. Before this, you need to seal the wood you have exposed in cutting the taper. Remember, this is the 'business end' of the stick, which will be constantly under threat from mud, muck and water. This process takes less than a minute and is well worth the effort. Any varnish will do, but I generally use the tin of yacht varnish I've bought to give the stick its final finish.

So, apply a little varnish (it need not dry off), replace the ferrule and tap it home so that it fits snugly against your earlier mark. To make sure it stays there, insert a small veneer pin (cut to length as necessary) near the rim of the ferrule, but at this stage do not tap the pin in completely. If you tie a loop of strong thread to the protruding pin, it will provide a convenient means of suspending the stick after it has been varnished, when leaving it to dry. Alternatively, use a small punch to create three equidistant dimples around the rim.

FINISHING

You must now apply a finish to the stick both to enhance and to protect it. Start by removing any accumulated grime or dirt. Using 0000 grade wire wool dipped in warm, soapy water, lightly rub down the stick, then wipe it clean and leave it to dry for half an hour.

Apply a coat of sanding sealer, sparingly, using a cloth dipped in the liquid. Leave this to dry for at least a couple of hours, then apply a first coat of yacht varnish diluted with white spirit (50:50) with a cloth or brush; the secret is not to put too much on and to avoid introducing foreign bodies like fluff and hair. Leave to dry in a warm room overnight.

Next, cut back the first coat very gently using 0000 grade wire wool, and wipe the stick clean, being careful to remove any wisps of wire wool. Then apply the second coat, this time of undiluted varnish. Leave it to dry as before, cut it back even more gently, wipe clean, and put on the final coat of undiluted varnish.

Once this has dried, the stick is ready for use.

Fig 2.15 *An unusually well-balanced thumbstick made from hazel.*

CHAPTER THREE

SIMPLE, ONE-PIECE WALKING STICKS

THERE are many types of one-piece walking sticks. All of those described here are easy to make and will help to develop your skills, knowledge and expertise.

Natural walking sticks.
Left: ash. Right: hazel.

| PROJECT | A CROSS-HEAD STICK |

A CROSS-HEAD STICK

Let us start with what is a very simple type of stick, but which, when properly trimmed and finished, is both attractive and comfortable to use: the cross-head stick.

SELECTING A STICK

The best examples of these, the most natural of all walking sticks, are difficult to find, but easy to produce. They are formed by a shank of sufficient length – minimum 36in (920mm) – growing at an angle of close to 90° from either the root or the branch of a tree. They can be found on most trees, certainly all of those described in Chapter 1, but the supply from some trees, notably hazel and ash, is more plentiful. It is also possible to grow them 'to order', particularly from young ash saplings. When one of these saplings is discovered, all but one of the strongest side shoots should be removed with a knife or secateurs (*see* Fig 3.1A). The plant should then be dug up carefully and the main stem cut back to about an inch (25mm) above the remaining side shoot. It should then be replanted on its side, 2–3in (51–76mm) below soil level, with the side shoot protruding above ground (*see* Fig 3.1B). This shoot will grow to form the main stem from which the shank will eventually be cut. If, during growth, side shoots start to develop on this stem, they should be removed immediately – and carefully.

When the stem is of sufficient length and diameter – about 1in (25mm) at ground level – the plant should again be lifted for trimming into a natural, and very strong, cross-head stick.

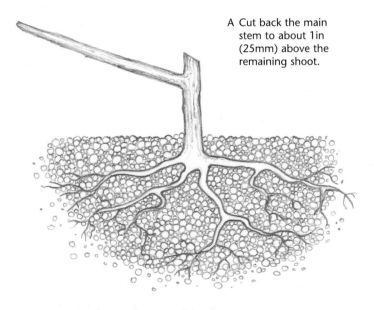

A Cut back the main stem to about 1in (25mm) above the remaining shoot.

Fig 3.1 *Growing a cross-head stick.*

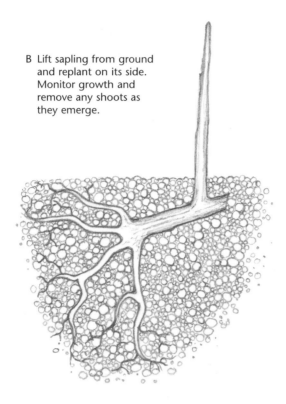

B Lift sapling from ground and replant on its side. Monitor growth and remove any shoots as they emerge.

FASHIONING THE STICK

For all cross-head sticks, it is important to cut the section which will form the handle overlong; this is true of any stick which is cut with branch or root attached. If, during seasoning, splits develop they can be removed in the final trimming process.

Producing the finished stick is largely a question of individual taste, but as a guide the shank length should be cut to approximately 36in (920mm) and the handle to about 4in (102mm). Any nodules on the shank or handle should be carefully removed and the stick cleaned prior to fitting a ferrule and applying varnish.

A KNOB STICK

In its most basic form, this is a shank with a lump of wood at the handle end taken from a branch, root or the trunk of a tree. Whilst it is important to ensure that the lump of wood from which the knob handle will be shaped is large enough for the purpose, the beauty of a knob stick is that, because the handle is relatively small and straightforward to produce, suitable shanks are easy to find. It is also the case that they can be made from sticks which were originally intended for a more ambitious project, but which went wrong at some stage in the making. I have salvaged several good knob sticks from intended Cardigan sticks (*see* Chapter 4) which developed a fault or were flawed.

PROJECT

SHAPING THE HANDLE

As to the shape of the knob, it can be left more or less in a natural form with minimal shaping or tidying up (*see* Fig 3.2), or a more stylized, rounded shape can be produced as I have done here.

In the first case, it is sufficient to dress the handle into a satisfying shape using a knife and sandpaper, whilst retaining its natural appearance. For a more stylized version, it is necessary to reduce the original lump of wood into something resembling a 2½in (64mm) cube (*see* Fig 3.3). A panel saw is perfectly adequate for this purpose although access to a power band saw makes the job quicker. Take care not to damage the bark when sawing the handle into its preliminary shape and remember to protect the shank with some form of sleeve if it is being held in a vice whilst being sawn (*see* page 18).

When the cube has been formed, draw the outline of the handle on to two opposite sides of the cube as in Fig 3.4. Some suggested profiles for knob handles are shown in Fig 3.5. Your choice of these, or such other variations as you desire, can be scaled up on a sheet of graph paper to finished dimensions. (*See* Fig 3.6.) Using carbon paper, transfer the selected shape to the cube, taking care that the outlines are in alignment with each other and with the shank. Remove surplus wood with a coping saw to give the rough shape, and then use a wood rasp or power file to remove all the sharp edges and produce a more rounded shape. In its finished form, this should not be perfectly circular, but have sides similar to a flattened sphere. Continue the shaping process until you are satisfied that the handle is symmetrical and sits well in the hand, using medium and then fine abrasive paper to refine the shape.

Fig 3.2 *A knob handle can be left more or less in its natural form.*

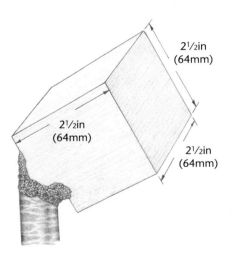

Fig 3.3 *Dimensions of block needed to produce a knob handle.*

2½in (64mm)

2½in (64mm)

2½in (64mm)

Fig 3.4 *Draw a rough outline of the shape desired onto the cube.*

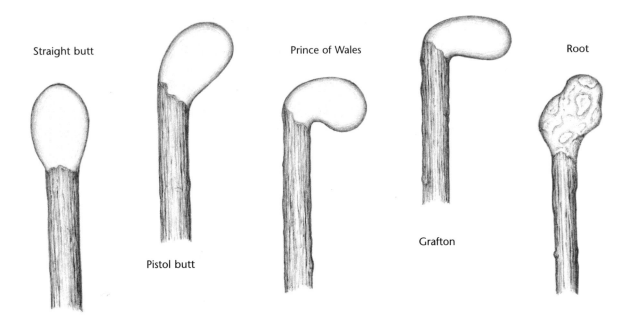

Straight butt

Pistol butt

Prince of Wales

Grafton

Root

Fig 3.5 *Examples of knob handle shapes.*

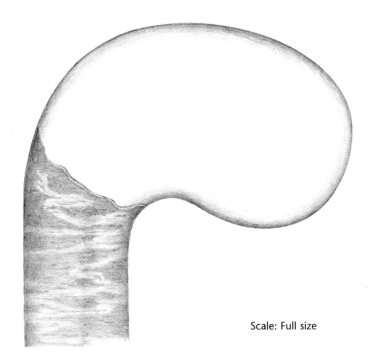

Scale: Full size

Fig 3.6 *Profile of finished knob stick.*

FINISHING THE STICK

The stick now needs to be cut to size, 36in (920mm) overall being the usual general purpose length. (*See* Chapter 4, page 42 for advice on how to cut a stick to suit a particular individual.) Once this has been done, fit a ferrule, then clean and varnish the stick as described in Chapter 2.

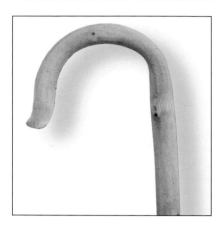

A ROUND-HANDLE STICK

The next stick we shall turn our attention to is the one most children would come up with if asked to draw a walking stick. Made in their thousands for the National Health Service in this country, round-handle sticks are to be found in most hospital out-patient departments and many 'country accessories' shops. They are a cheap and functional aid to walking with few pretensions beyond that.

Ash and sweet chestnut are the woods normally used for the commercial production of such sticks. In the case of ash the bark is normally left on the shank, whilst sticks made from sweet chestnut can be stripped and coloured.

SHAPING THE HANDLE

To produce the round handle two things are required. The first is a means of heating that part of the stick which is to be bent – usually the last 15in (381mm) of the handle end of the shank. The second is a former or jig, around which the handle can be bent and held in place until it sets. Producing a suitable jig, such as the one shown in Fig 3.7, is straight-forward, but will take longer than making the stick itself! Once made, however, the jig can be used to produce however many sticks are required.

The details of the jig are shown in Fig 3.7. The backplate and bending roll are best made from scraps of hardwood (mine are oak and mahogany respectively) in order to sustain the pressure being exerted on them. The 'stop', shown below the roll, is a 5in (127mm) long steel coach bolt, ³⁄₈in (10mm) in diameter, the threaded section of which has been cut off to avoid the threads marking the stick as it is bent.

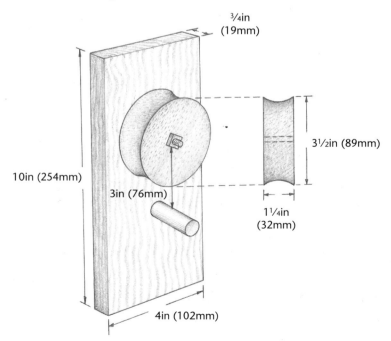

Fig 3.7 *A bending jig used to produce round-handle sticks.*

As to the method of heating the stick, there are several options available, from the traditional method of a tray of hot damp sand to the more modern hot air stripper. Both of these have disadvantages; the former is cumbersome to construct and house, whilst with the latter, distributing and maintaining a consistent heat is difficult to achieve. My preference for generating the necessary heat, safely and conveniently, is the electrically powered water boiler I described in Chapter 2 (*see* page 17). Several handles can be heated simultaneously or the odd one included with sticks being treated for straightening.

To make a stick of this type it is necessary to start with a straight shank around 48in (1,200mm) in length and 1in (25mm) in diameter. Cut a shallow notch about ½in (12mm) in from the handle end and tie a 15in (381mm) length of strong string onto it so that the two ends of the string are of equal length. The tails of string thus produced will eventually be used to secure the handle in place.

Next, put the handle end in to steam for up to an hour, covering it with sacking or something similar to contain the heat around the area that is to be bent. It is impossible to be more precise about the length of time needed to heat the stick adequately. There are so many variables that only practice will tell you how long. If, on trial, the stick doesn't bend immediately, do not force it – it will crack. Put it back in to steam for a little longer and then try again.

You now have to work quickly to avoid excessive heat loss from the stick. Place the heated end between the stop and the bending roll, and take the shank in a clockwise direction around the bending roll, keeping it tight on the roll (*see* Fig 3.8). Tie the string firmly around the shank at a point in line with the notched end (*see* Fig 3.9). Until you feel confident, it will help if you enlist a second pair of hands to tie off the string whilst you are holding the stick under tension.

Fig 3.8 *Curling the shank round the bending roll.*

Fig 3.9 *Tying string round the stick to keep it tight on the bending roll.*

Fig 3.10 The stick, complete with bending roll, is removed from the jig and stored overnight.

This bending process may cause some slivers to spring from the crown of the handle: don't worry, we will deal with these shortly.

The stick, complete with bending roll, can now be removed from the jig and stored overnight to allow the handle to set firmly (*see* Fig 3.10). The next day cut away the string, which will cause the handle to spring back a little, and gently ease out the bending roll. To help set it even further, a hot air gun may be played over the area of the handle for 2–3 minutes.

FINISHING THE HANDLE

To produce the finished handle, there are two options. You may simply cut off the notch end, rounding it with sandpaper to give a conventional handle, or you may leave it slightly longer, tapering the end with a knife and file to produce the basic shape of the turned-out nose found on traditional crooks (*see* Fig 3.11). Indeed, the method presented here for a round-handle stick is one way to produce a traditional crook. By selecting a longer shank initially – minimum of 60in (1,500mm) will be needed – and following exactly the same process, a rudimentary crook can be made (*see* Fig 3.12).

Having produced the shape of your choice you now need to tidy up any loose slivers on the outer surface of the handle. Using a sharp knife and working with the grain, carefully cut away any slivers at their base and gently sand down with fine abrasive paper.

FINISHING THE STICK

If you have elected to leave the bark on the stick, it may have wrinkled on the inside radius of the handle. This is very difficult to prevent and the only way to remove it is by stripping the bark from the handle which may then be coloured or left natural before cleaning, varnishing and fitting a ferrule to complete the stick.

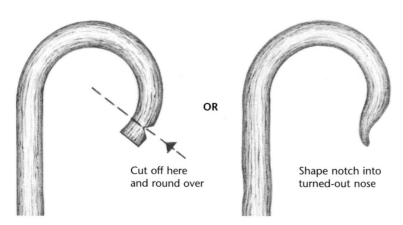

Cut off here
and round over

OR

Shape notch into
turned-out nose

Fig 3.11 The two options for finishing a turned-out nose.

Fig 3.12 A rudimentary crook.

COLOURING TECHNIQUES

The bark can be stripped from any stick and the resultant surface coloured by staining, fuming or scorching.

STAINING

If you decide to stain a stick with a commercial product, try the colour on an offcut first. Inevitably, it will differ from the shade shown on the tin. It is better to start with a light stain and darken it, if necessary, by applying additional coats, than to produce something which is immediately darker than you wanted. Remember that stains quickly penetrate the surface of raw wood and cannot easily be wiped off if the effect is not what you expected. So, experiment first.

FUMING

The traditional technique of fuming is another method of colouring wood. It takes longer, and the extra work involved may not suit the impatient, but the results can be effective.

Fuming requires an infusion of bark peelings with boiling water to be made. This, when cold, is wiped over the peeled stick. The stick should then be suspended in a suitable length of plastic rainwater pipe, with a polythene bag tied in place on the top end to seal it.

Position the pipe so it is resting vertically, place a small container of ammonium below the bottom end, and leave the stick to stew in the ammonia fumes. Check the progress after a couple of hours, and when the colouration is to your satisfaction, remove the stick from the ammonia. Leave it to dry out completely, then gently rub in linseed oil with 0000 grade wire wool to bring out the finish.

If you are going to try this technique, only do so out of doors, and carefully observe the manufacturer's instructions for handling and disposing of the ammonia.

SCORCHING

Scorching is a method used to bring out the grain on a peeled stick. It requires the use of a concentrated, clean flame, such as that from a gas blowlamp of the type used to strip paint. The stick should be clamped securely and the flame played along its length until it singes the surface of the wood. Do not keep the flame in the one spot for too long and avoid burning the wood – the object is to highlight the grain pattern, not to convert the stick into charcoal!

When the desired effect has been achieved, rub the stick down lightly with wire wool and apply a protective varnish finish.

FIRST STEPS IN CARVING

To round off this chapter I thought it would be fun, by means of basic woodcarving steps, to convert the knob stick described earlier into something a little more ambitious: for example, a duck's head.

We start by taking the shape of the finished knob stick (*see* Fig 3.6), which is virtually the side profile of the head (minus the beak) we want to create. Viewed from the front, however, a duck's head is quite a different shape. The dome is much narrower than the beak area and there is a groove running from the eye towards the beak. These differences can clearly be seen in Fig 3.13.

SHAPING THE HEAD

Because we are going to add the beak later we can ignore it for the time being. We will start by marking some pencil lines on the head to give us a guide to the eventual shape and provide a basis for removing the surplus wood. Using Fig 3.14 as a guide, draw in lines A, B and C and cut along them with a coping saw to convert the knob handle into something which is immediately more duck-like in appearance. Then, draw in the guidelines D and E on the top of the head and cut along these to reduce the cheeks of the duck to more lifelike proportions.

The next stage is to start shaping the contours of the head. Begin by drawing in two guidelines on top of the head as in Fig 3.15. These are intended to identify the dome of the head and will help you position the groove which runs from eye to beak. Using a ³⁄₈in (10mm), half-round rasp, shape the cheek area on both sides of the head so that it tapers upwards towards the pencil marks. Start by using the flat face of the rasp

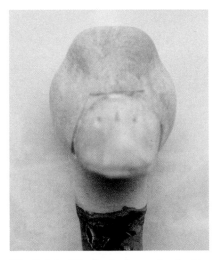

Fig 3.13 *The basic shape of a duck's head handle: note the narrow dome and grooves running from eyes to beak.*

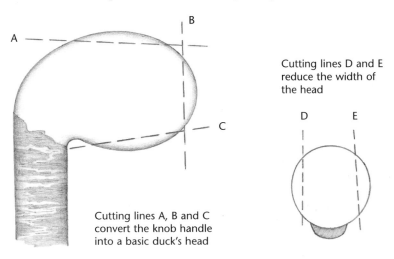

Cutting lines D and E reduce the width of the head

Cutting lines A, B and C convert the knob handle into a basic duck's head

Fig 3.14 *Cutting lines to convert a knob handle to a basic duck's head shape.*

and then, as the head takes shape, use the round face to make an indentation in both cheeks to represent the eye grooves (*see* Fig 3.15). When you are satisfied with the appearance and symmetry of the head, leave it. Do not, at this stage, attempt to bring it to its finished shape; this is left until the beak is in place, which is the next step.

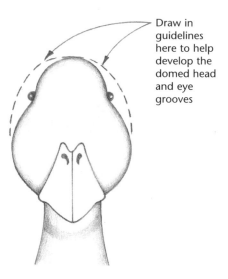

Draw in guidelines here to help develop the domed head and eye grooves

MAKING THE BEAK

The beak can be produced from any one of several materials depending on the variety of duck you intend to represent. I have used buffalo horn, cow horn, antler and different types of wood, but my preference is for ram's horn; its translucence, grain and colours give it a most natural appearance.

Whatever material you choose, it first needs to be cut into a rough wedge approximately 2 x 1¼ x ¾in (51 x 32 x 19mm), and the thick end reduced to a circular dowel approximately ½in (12mm) long and ⅜in (10mm) in diameter. Alternatively, a short bolt may be used in place of the dowel (*see* Fig 3.16). Drill a ⅜in (10mm) hole, approximately ½in (12mm) deep, at the centre front of the head and try the beak for fit (*see* Fig 3.17). Clean up the joint area of the dome and cheeks with abrasive paper before setting the beak in place with glue. I generally use two-tube epoxy resin and keep the joint tight overnight with a small G-cramp.

When the glue has set, the beak can be filed to shape until you are satisfied with the balance, conformation and overall appearance of the head. Any file marks should then be sanded out by hand and final adjustments made to the shape. (See Fig 3.19.)

Fig 3.15 Shaping the contours of the duck's head.

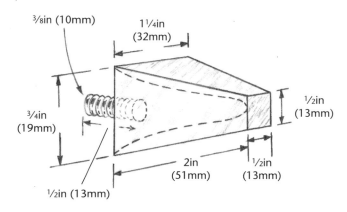

⅜in (10mm)

1¼in (32mm)

Exact dimensions will be determined by the size of the head, but should be in the region of those shown here

¾in (19mm)

½in (13mm)

2in (51mm)

½in (13mm)

½in (13mm)

Fig 3.16 Wedge for beak made from horn.

POSITIONING THE EYES

What now remains is to decide how faithfully you wish to represent a duck's head, for this will determine how much detail needs to be included. If this is your first attempt at carving, then I recommend you keep it simple. As long as *you* are satisfied with the product it doesn't really matter if it isn't ornithologically perfect; your ability to achieve such detail will increase and improve with experience.

Fig 3.17 *Trying the beak for fit.*

Fig 3.18 *The duck's head with the beak joint sanded and the beak glued in place.*

Fig 3.19 *The beak filed to shape and sanded.*

As a minimum, you need to include eyes. These can be painted on, burned in or suitable glass ones bought and glued in. (*See* Fig 3.20.) Positioning the eyes is important – if they are not correctly positioned they will spoil the whole effect. They should be in the same position on either side of the head! Determining the precise location really requires some field research, but in the absence of the real thing I recommend that you imagine the main section of the head (excluding the beak) is based on a grid of nine squares. The centre of the eye should be in the top left-hand corner of the centre square. (*See* Fig 3.21.)

With the eyes in place, the head and beak can be coloured, wax polished or varnished to achieve the amount of detail you desire.

Fig 3.20 *The head with glass eyes fixed in position.*

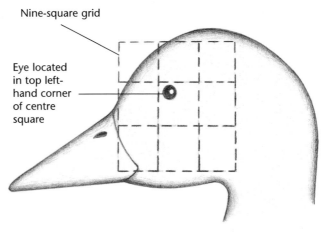

Nine-square grid

Eye located
in top left-
hand corner
of centre
square

Fig 3.21 *Locating the eyes.*

CHAPTER FOUR

CARDIGAN STICKS

ONE of the sticks I obtain most satisfaction from making is that known locally as a Cardigan stick, sometimes called a Llandovery stick. Named after the area in which it was first developed, it may indeed have been the type of stick carried by drovers who walked with herds of cattle from this part of Wales to the markets in central and southern England. As a child I certainly remember a great-uncle of mine, who must then have been in his seventies, carrying a stick of this type. He owned a cob stallion which he would walk around the farms of west Wales to serve the resident mares. This circular tour covered a hundred miles (170km) or more and was completed by the early part of the year when he was able to cut sufficient supplies of sticks to work on during the winter months. The profile of the stick handle in Fig 4.1 is taken from the last stick my uncle ever made.

Cardigan stick made from a branch of hazel.

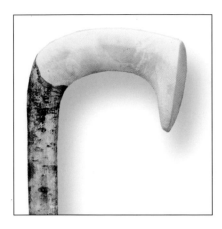

A ONE-PIECE CARDIGAN STICK

The critical thing in making this stick is to find a suitable shank growing from a branch (or, though less frequently, from a root) at an appropriate angle. If the angle is either too wide or too narrow, whilst it may be suitable for other projects it will not make a good Cardigan stick.

SELECTING A SUITABLE SHANK

In the example in Fig 4.2A, the handle would have to be cut from the diameter of the branch, which would be insufficiently wide to offer a handle of comfortable length in the finished walking stick. Whilst it would be possible to cut a handle of sufficient length from the branch shown in Fig 4.2B, to do so would mean taking it to the outer limit of the circumference of the branch. This then poses two difficulties:

1 the width of the section of branch at that point may not provide enough wood from which to shape a pleasing handle; and
2 even if it does, the handle will give the appearance of running too far into the shank (*see* Fig 4.3).

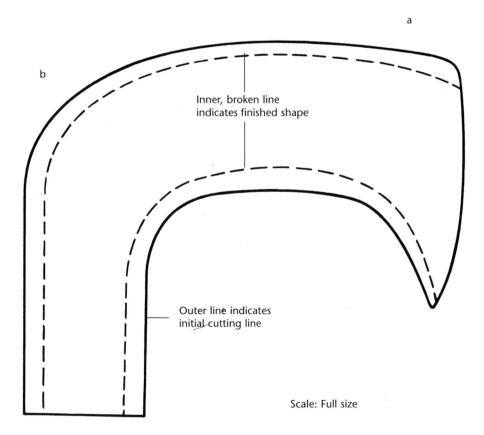

Inner, broken line indicates finished shape

Outer line indicates initial cutting line

Scale: Full size

Fig 4.1 *Profile of handle for Cardigan stick.*

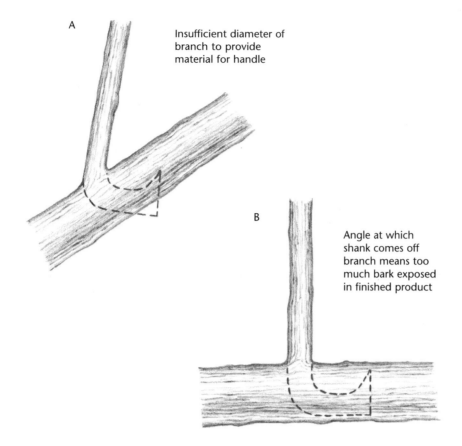

A

Insufficient diameter of
branch to provide
material for handle

B

Angle at which
shank comes off
branch means too
much bark exposed
in finished product

Fig 4.2 *Problems to avoid in selecting suitable shanks.*

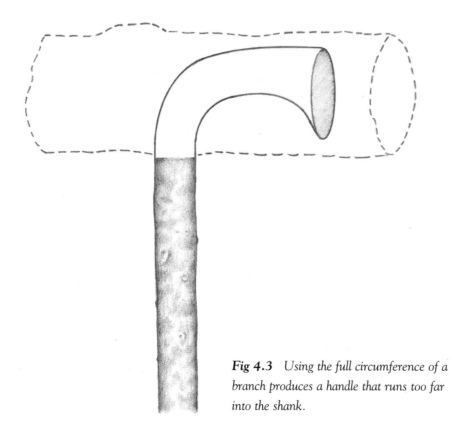

Fig 4.3 *Using the full circumference of a branch produces a handle that runs too far into the shank.*

For an everyday stick there may be nothing wrong with that, but in the best examples of this type of stick, the bark should be left on the shank to the point where the handle starts its right angle bend (*see* Fig 4.4). I suppose one might argue that if the bark is to be removed entirely from the stick, then it really doesn't matter. Whilst that may be true, I have never seen a Cardigan stick in its 'naked form' and I do not believe it would do anything for its appearance.

Fig 4.4 *Generally, the bark is left on up to the bend in the handle.*

What we are searching for as an ideal starting point is the example shown in Fig 4.5. Here it will be relatively easy to find sufficient length, width and depth to work with at the point where the potential shank meets the branch of the tree.

In theory, a Cardigan stick can be made from any type of tree which offers the conformation of branch and shank I have just described. In practice, virtually all of the one-piece Cardigan sticks I have made come from hazel wood. Not only does hazel offer consistently good examples of what we are looking for, but the combinations of attractive bark on the shank and grain configurations on the finished handle are difficult to beat.

I am often asked by other stickmakers 'Why waste a shank making a Cardigan stick when it could be better used to make a market stick or crook?' The answer is simple – I only use those shanks which are not going to be long enough to make anything else for Cardigan sticks. It is often the case that I find something growing which at first sight appears suitable for making a crook, but which, on closer examination reveals a flaw in the shank or branch. Though ruling it out for my first intention, this still provides material from which a perfectly acceptable alternative can be produced, and none more so than a Cardigan stick.

Dimensions for the finished stick can be taken from Fig 4.1. The only additional observation I would make is that the handle should taper gently from point a to point b as shown in Fig 4.6. In the case of a gent's stick, if the dimension at a is 1½in (38mm) then at b it should be 1¼in (32mm); for a lady's stick, if a is 1¼in (32mm), then b should be 1⅛in (29mm). To obtain these finished dimensions, it is necessary to start with something in the order of Fig 4.7.

Fig 4.5 *An example of a shank with good potential for a Cardigan stick.*

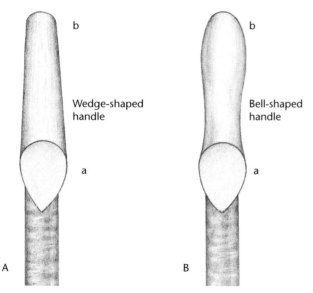

Wedge-shaped handle

Bell-shaped handle

b

b

a

a

A

B

Fig 4.6 *The handle should have a gentle taper from point a to b.*

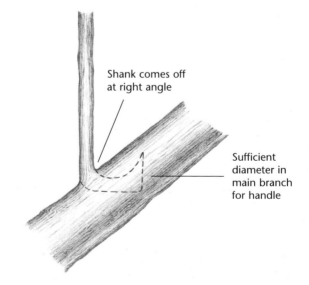

Shank comes off at right angle

Sufficient diameter in main branch for handle

Fig 4.7 *The shank configuration required to produce a satisfactory Cardigan stick.*

KNOW YOUR MATERIAL

Having cut, trimmed and seasoned the piece in line with the advice in Chapter 1, it is now time to start working on it. Your first step should be to look critically at the piece you are about to start shaping in the way a woodcarver or sculptor would. Handle it, turn it over and imagine, referring to the photograph on page 33, what the finished stick – particularly the handle – should look like. This should give you a feel for the wood and should help you to see, in your mind's eye, what it is you are trying to produce. This is an important stage; do not overlook it.

INITIAL SHAPING

The next step is to convert the round branch which will form the handle into a flat, rectangular block (*see* Fig 4.8). To achieve this, make two longitudinal cuts with a small axe or panel saw as shown in Fig 4.9. These must be parallel to the shank and should be made so that they produce a block which has a minimum width of 2in (51mm). The length and depth of the block will, of course, be determined by the shape of the branch from which the block has first been cut. At this stage there is no need to do any more to the block – any surplus wood will be removed as we start to shape the handle.

DRAWING THE HANDLE

Now we need to transfer the outline of the handle using a template taken from the profile shown in Fig 4.1 (*see* page 34). I generally cut my templates from pieces of waste plastic containers that I save for the purpose. Plastic is more durable than cardboard, but any piece of stiff cardboard will do if nothing stronger comes to hand.

Having trimmed and cut out your template, place it in position on the block at a right angle to the shank, as shown in Fig 4.10. Hold it firmly and draw round it in pencil (*see* Fig 4.11). It is not necessary to draw the outline on both sides of the block.

If you are satisfied with the way the handle looks in relation to the shank, you can now start to cut away some of the surplus wood from the block.

CUTTING OUT THE HANDLE

A word of warning here. Even if you have access to a power band saw or jigsaw, do not, under any circumstances, cut round the outlined handle in one attempt. If you do so, and are subsequently dissatisfied with the resulting shape, you are left with very little room for manoeuvre.

Initially, remove only the wood from the area below the handle. Mark in some guidelines (as shown in Fig 4.12) and make a series of saw cuts at, approximately, ¼in (6mm) intervals, parallel with the shank, stopping just short of the bottom line of the handle (*see* Fig 4.13). This wood can

Fig 4.8 *To make the handle, the round branch is first transformed into a flat, rectangular block.*

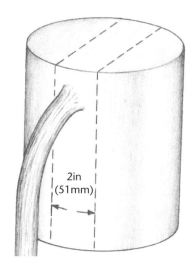

Fig 4.9 *Guidelines for the two longitudinal cuts.*

2in
(51mm)

Fig 4.10 *Marking the handle shape outline onto the block.*

Fig 4.11 *Draw the handle at right angles to the shank.*

Fig 4.12 *Mark in guidelines for removing the wood from the area below the handle.*

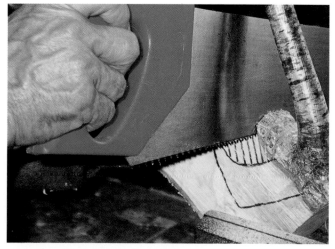

Fig 4.13 *Cut along the guidelines, stopping just short of the bottom line of the handle.*

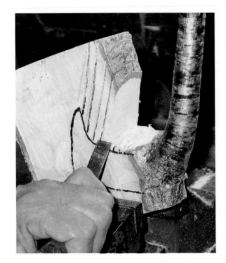

Fig 4.14 *Remove the wood with a chisel and mallet.*

Fig 4.15 *File any remaining stumps down to the line of the handle.*

Fig 4.16 *Remove the waste from the top line of the handle with a panel saw or power jigsaw.*

then be removed with a wood chisel and mallet. Remember to attack the cuts from both sides of the block to minimize the risk of pieces breaking off where they shouldn't. (*See* Fig 4.14.)

Clean up this area with a round wood rasp or, if you have one, a power file. You can now take any remaining stumps left by the saw and chisel cuts down to the line of the handle (*see* Fig 4.15). Do so carefully. Whilst it is not necessary to attempt to get the line and shape exactly right now, remember that this will be the baseline for the other cuts you make to shape the rest of the handle.

Once you are satisfied with the bottom line of the handle, use a panel saw or power jigsaw to remove the waste from the top line of the handle (*see* Fig 4.16). Follow the line as closely as you can, but, so long as you don't bite into the area to be used for the handle, don't worry about producing a perfectly symmetrical line. You will need to achieve that when you shape the handle into its final form.

Pause to consider the handle which is starting to develop. How does it look, is it symmetrical, is it likely to fit into the hand? You need to be satisfied, for this is the final opportunity you have to make adjustments before removing the waste wood still remaining. Although the bottom line of the handle has already been determined, the top line can still be extended if you think it will produce a more comfortable stick (*see* Fig 4.17). Whilst it is usual for the end of the handle to be cut parallel to the shank, it is quite acceptable for the top line to extend beyond the bottom, thus producing an angled cut to the end. Once you have made your decision, use a panel saw to remove the remaining waste (*see* Fig 4.18). You should now be holding a stick similar to the example shown in Fig 4.19.

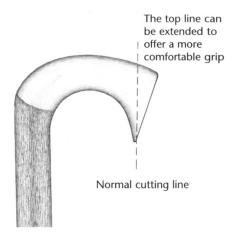

The top line can be extended to offer a more comfortable grip

Normal cutting line

Fig 4.17 *Adjust the top line of the handle to produce a comfortable stick.*

Fig 4.18 *With the final decision on the shape of handle made, remove the remaining waste.*

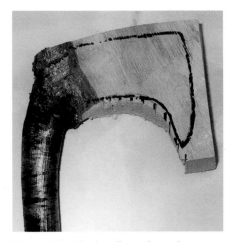

Fig 4.19 *The handle outline after initial rough shaping.*

What remains is to shape the handle into something which both feels good and looks good. You should be trying to produce a handle which, in cross section, has the shape of an inverted egg (*see* Fig 4.20) and in plan, tapers slightly from the end towards the top of the shank (*see* Fig 4.6). For your first attempt, I recommend that this taper is in the form of a straightforward wedge (*see* Fig 4.6A). With more experience, however, you can develop a more interesting (and more comfortable) elongated bell-shape (*see* Fig 4.6B). It isn't that much more difficult to produce and it certainly makes for a better stick.

SHAPING THE HANDLE

With the final shape fixed in your mind, start to convert what is still a fairly square section of handle into something more oval. Initially, I recommend that you use a variety of rasps, differing in width and roughness, to remove the bulk of the waste (*see* Figs 4.21 and 4.22). Pause frequently to contemplate progress; this is the critical stage when it is all too easy to take off too much and spoil the effect you are looking for. So, caution is the order of the day.

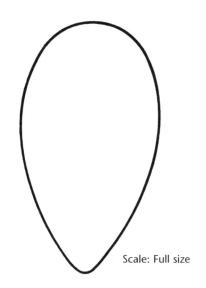

Scale: Full size

Fig 4.20 *Cross section of finished handle end.*

Fig 4.21 *Remove most of the waste with a variety of rasps . . .*

Fig 4.22 *. . . being careful not to remove too much in one go.*

41

Fig 4.23 Smooth out any rasp marks with a scraper, working in the direction of the grain.

Fig 4.24 A stick that fits its owner!

When you believe that you are getting close to the final shape, put down the rasps. The graze marks left by the rasps now have to be smoothed out, and for this task you will need some form of scraper. Working carefully in the direction of the grain, and with minimum pressure, draw the scraper over any rasp marks until they disappear (*see* Fig 4.23).

The handle now needs to be smoothed down with abrasive paper, using a fairly coarse grade to start (say P100), then medium (P180) and a finer grade (such as P280) to finish. You should continue sanding until all blemishes are removed and any grain configuration becomes clear. The final smoothing process, to remove any scratch marks left by sanding, should be completed using 0000 grade steel wool.

CUTTING THE SHANK TO LENGTH

It is now time to cut the shank to the desired length before fitting a ferrule. If the stick is being tailor-made for someone, you should involve them in the decision making! Invite them, with their walking shoes on, to hold the stick, and note the angle of the elbow. If it is too bent, the stick is too long; if the elbow is straight, then the stick is already too short! What you're aiming for, remember, is something which will facilitate the process of walking. A comfortable stick becomes an extension of your hand and, when you use it, you should not really be aware that it's there. One which is too long will become tiring to use, whilst one which is too short will fail to provide you with the necessary lift. Figure 4.24 shows a stick cut to the length which suits its user.

If the stick is not intended for a particular person, then I recommend that you keep it at the standard length of 36in (91cm). While this, in practice, may be too long for many people, it is easy to reduce the length, but the converse is not true.

Whatever length you decide on, remember to cut the shank with a fine-toothed saw and protect the bark if the stick is being held in a vice. With the shank length fixed, fit the ferrule, then clean and varnish the stick as described in Chapter 2.

CHAPTER FIVE

WOODEN CROOKS AND MARKET STICKS

IN producing this type of stick, the first decision we have to take is whether to make it from a single piece of wood or to shape the handle from a separate block and graft it on to a suitable shank. The finished products are equally pleasing and each has its supporters and critics.

A good starting point is to identify the difference between a crook and a market stick. Originally, this was quite straightforward: a crook was very much a working tool used by shepherds to catch sheep, while a market stick was a more embellished product to be shown off on market days and special occasions. Over the years, however, this simple differentiation has become blurred.

Whilst it is true that market sticks have remained largely unchanged, crooks are now being shaped, carved and coloured to the point where many will never be seen by a sheep and will certainly never be used to stop one on the charge!

A simpler way to distinguish between them these days is by the length of the shank. Remembering their original purpose, crooks will always be longer than market sticks: about 52in (1,300mm) in total compared with around 48in (1,200mm) for a typical market stick.

A well-turned one-piece crook in hazel.

A ONE-PIECE WOODEN MARKET STICK

I have chosen to start with this stick because many of the techniques involved have already been introduced in earlier chapters. The profile of the stick we are going to make, described as a 'nose-in' variety, is shown in Fig 5.1. To produce it we need to obtain a shank of suitable length: a minimum of 48in (1,200mm), growing from a branch or root of acceptable diameter – about 4in (102mm) – at a satisfactory angle, say 40°. Figure 5.2 shows a good example of what we are looking for, cut from hazel.

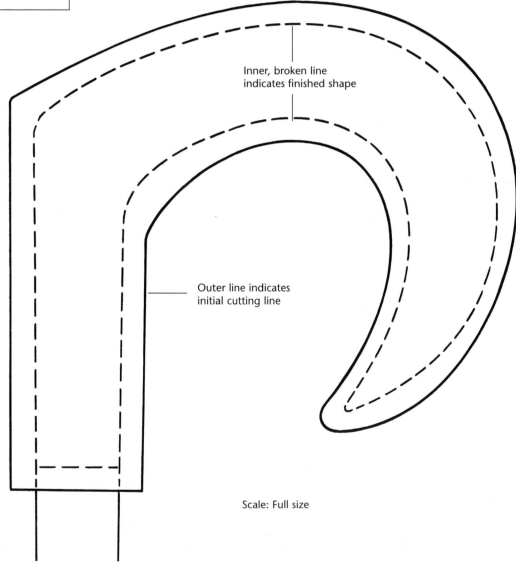

Inner, broken line
indicates finished shape

Outer line indicates
initial cutting line

Scale: Full size

Fig 5.1 *Profile of nose-in market stick.*

SHAPING THE HANDLE

After seasoning, the block from which the handle will be made needs to be squared off using exactly the same method as was used to produce the Cardigan stick (*see* Chapter 4, page 39). The outline of the handle should then be transferred to one face of the block (*see* Fig 5.3). Use a template cut from stiff card or plastic, based on the design in Fig 5.1, to do this.

Fig 5.2 *A shank with the potential for a one-piece market stick.*

Fig 5.3 *Mark the outline of the handle onto one face of the squared-off block.*

Remove surplus wood with a coping saw, jigsaw or band saw, first cutting the bottom line of the handle with a series of saw cuts and a chisel, as for the Cardigan stick (*see* page 40), and only then taking out the waste from above the handle (*see* Fig 5.4). Using a series of rasps, all square edges should then be taken off to produce a round handle with a diameter of about 1in (25mm). The nose of the handle should be shaped to a blunt point (*see* Fig 5.5).

Fig 5.4 *Remove the waste from the bottom line of the handle before moving to the waste wood above the top line.*

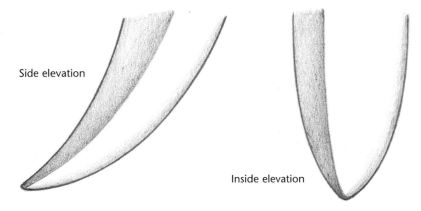

Side elevation

Inside elevation

Fig 5.5 *The shaping required for a nose-in market stick handle.*

FINISHING

When you are satisfied with the symmetry and feel of the handle, the rasp marks should be removed by scraping and sanding to produce the final surface. The shank should then be cut back to 48in (1,200mm), if it is overlong, and cleaned before it is fitted with a ferrule and varnished.

A ONE-PIECE WOODEN CROOK

PROJECT

A well-finished crook made from a single piece of hazel is the most beautifully functional stick one can own. It calls out to be used and it matters not whether it is used for its traditional purpose or as a fashion accessory in the pages of glossy 'country' magazines.

At first sight the outline of a crook appears standardized, but this is far from the truth. The shape and balance of the handle of a good crook is what sets it apart from others, and whilst there are few cardinal rules governing shape and dimensions, it is all too easy to spoil a crook by getting its relationships wrong. What do I mean by 'relationships'? Let's look at some examples by referring to Fig 5.6.

A The crown of the handle should never droop – it will make the whole stick appear to sag. On the other hand, it is quite acceptable for it to kick upwards a little.

B The gape is traditionally said to be four fingers wide which, allowing for differences in finger width, converts to approximately 3½in (89mm).

C The heel of the stick should not be too thick in comparison with both the neck and crown.

D Whilst the balance of a crook is difficult to define absolutely, a good way to test it is by holding it by one hand, about one-third of the length down from the ferrule end. At that point, which is where a shepherd would hold it to catch a sheep, it should not feel as if the handle is weighing it heavily towards the ground.

E It is said that the original function of the turned-out nose of a crook was to allow a shepherd to hook a lantern on it when ministering to a sheep at night. If that is so, then a half-curled nose (*see* Fig 5.7) would not have been functional, though for all other purposes it is perfectly acceptable.

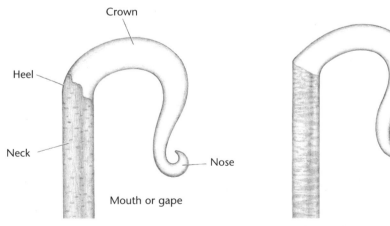

Fig 5.6 *The various parts of a crook in relation to one another.*

Fig 5.7 *A half-curled nose.*

We will return to the question of relationships and look at some additional considerations when we make a two-piece crook (*see* page 55). To make our first crook in wood, the profile and dimensions shown in Fig 5.8 will satisfy the accepted conventions and produce a pleasing shape.

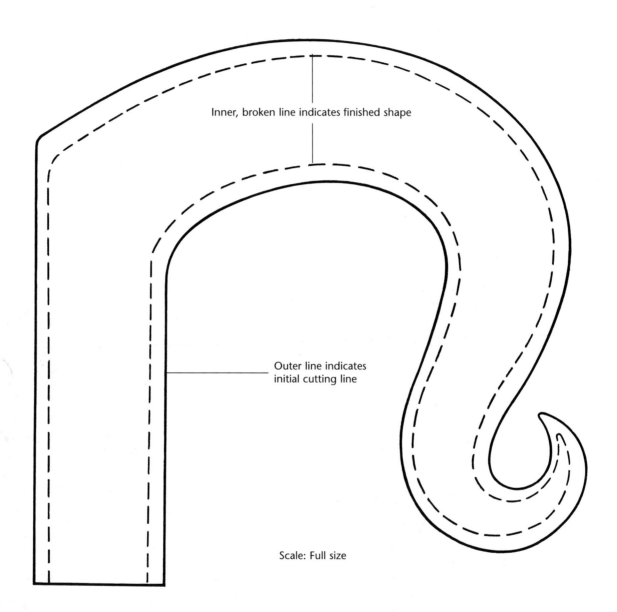

Inner, broken line indicates finished shape

Outer line indicates
initial cutting line

Scale: Full size

Fig 5.8 *Template for crook.*

SELECTING A SUITABLE SHANK

The processes involved in making a one-piece crook are very similar to those just described for a market stick.

Again, the starting point is the most important – finding a suitable shank attached to an acceptable branch or root. This time, however, our task is made more difficult by the fact that the shank has to be longer: 52in (1,300mm) is about right. The diameter of the branch or root should be around 4in (102mm) and the angle at which the shank joins the branch should be approximately 35°. Figure 5.9 illustrates the importance of a configuration which will permit the formation of the crook handle.

SHAPING THE HANDLE

When the wood has been seasoned the first step, as with the market stick, is to square off the branch or root section into a block to take the outline of the handle. This 'blank' should take the shape of the example shown in Fig 5.10, the dimensions of which should be around 7 x 5 x 1½in (178 x 127 x 38mm).

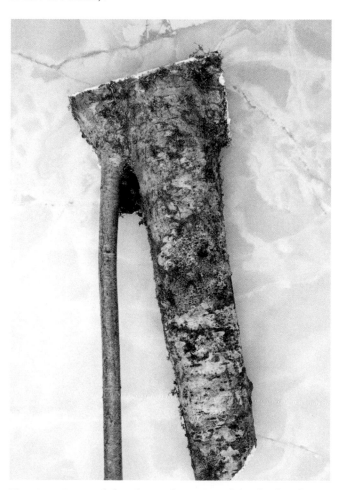

Fig 5.9 *It is vital that the configuration of the shank will allow the formation of the crook handle.*

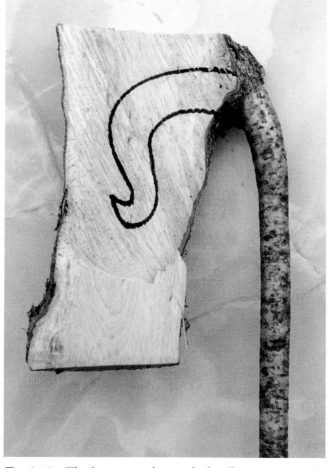

Fig 5.10 *The first step in shaping the handle is to square-off the branch or root section.*

Having transferred the outline to the block, using a template based on Fig 5.8, mark in guidelines for cutting below the handle and proceed to remove surplus wood as before (*see* page 40). Get into the habit of removing the wood from below before you start to take off the waste from above (*see* Figs 5.11 and 5.12). This is good practice. When you begin to design your own profiles, you should always start by drawing, and subsequently cutting, the bottom or inside line of the handle. If you do it the other way round, i.e. by starting with the top or outside line, I guarantee the crook will never look right. This is the case when drawing and cutting all handles, but is particularly so with crooks which have a turned-out nose.

When you have removed all of the waste, round over the square edges, using a succession of rasps, until you have reduced the handle to a diameter equivalent to that of the shank where it originally joined the block, tapering it gradually until it reaches a blunt point at the nose. The object is to produce a nicely rounded effect avoiding, if at all possible, surfaces which are flat, so that the line and contours of the handle flow from heel to nose.

FINISHING

Rasp marks should be removed with scrapers and abrasive paper before you fit a ferrule and varnish.

Fig 5.11 *Always remove the wood from below the handle . . .*

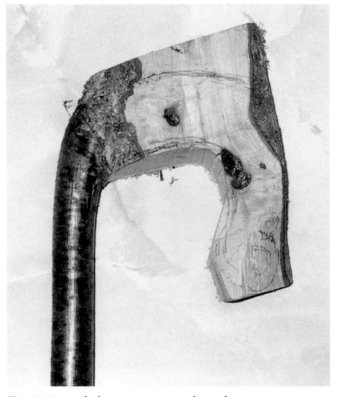

Fig 5.12 *. . . before removing any from above.*

A TWO-PIECE WOODEN MARKET STICK

The great advantage of a two-piece stick is that you are not bound by the limitations of shape, colour and dimension which are presented by the configuration of the natural material in a one-piece stick. You may use whatever wood your heart desires (and your pocket can afford!) for the handle, and its design can be as simple or as complex as your ambition determines.

The main disadvantage, of course, is that the handle has to be attached to the shank. This itself is not difficult, but no matter how the handle is cut from a block of wood, the direction of the grain can result in the creation of weak spots (*see* Fig 5.13). Whilst this may not be critical in the case of a stick intended only for walking or showing, such weaknesses would immediately be exposed, for example, in a crook being used to restrain a sheep! One way to reduce, if not eliminate, such risks is to make the handle from a piece of wood which is naturally bent to a shape close to that you are seeking to produce. In this case, the grain follows the line of the handle rather than running across it at any point and this adds to its strength. Although you will be very fortunate to find a piece capable of producing a full crook handle, it is much easier to come across pieces from which smaller, market stick handles can be formed: Fig 5.14 shows some examples. These may not produce such showy handles as those cut from carefully selected blocks, but they will certainly be stronger in use.

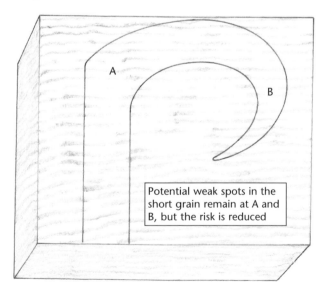

Potential weak spots in the short grain remain at A and B, but the risk is reduced

Fig 5.13 *Positioning the handle outline on the block to minimize weak spots.*

Fig 5.14 *Branches with the potential for producing successful market stick handles.*

SHAPING THE HANDLE

For the two-piece stick we are going to make, I have decided to use a block of sycamore for the handle. This is a clean, close-grained wood, light in colour, easy to work and durable. The minimum block size we shall need is 6 x 6 x 1¼in (152 x 152 x 32mm). Such blocks can be cut from the larger planks readily obtainable from timber merchants or wood mills.

The profile for the handle is shown in Fig 5.1. By transferring this to Perspex or other stiff, transparent material, and laying it on the block, you will be able to note the direction of the grain and decide the optimum position. Remember, too, that by adjusting positions it might be possible to cut more than one handle from the block – particularly important when expensive hardwoods are being used. When I am cutting a handle like this, I prefer to see the grain running through it, as shown in Fig 5.13. With the grain in this direction, the risk of weak spots at points A and B is reduced.

Having decided on the best position, draw a pencil line round the template and use a coping saw or fine band saw to cut out the shape. Select a suitable shank to match the wood being used for the handle. This is very much a matter of personal choice – I prefer to go for a contrast between the two. For a sycamore handle, therefore, I would choose a darker type of hazel shank or one with a pronounced mottled effect. For a market stick, remember, the shank would have to be around 48in (1,200mm) long.

When you have made your selection, you have also effectively determined the diameter to which you will need to reduce your handle. As before, use rasps or a power file to round over the edges until you have brought the diameter of the neck of the handle to about ⅛in (3mm) larger than the diameter of the top of the shank. For the moment, stop filing.

FITTING HANDLE TO SHANK

The next stage is to fit the handle to the shank – a process known as 'shanking'. There are several methods which can be used. For joining wood to wood, I prefer to make a dowel on the shank which fits tightly into a socket drilled into the handle, and then to glue it in place (*see* Fig 5.15). It is important that the dowel marries up with the socket correctly so that the handle, when fitted, is in alignment with the shank and the joint thus formed is clean and tight. Patience is needed to get this part of the process absolutely right; a poor joint will spoil an otherwise perfect stick.

To make the dowel, mark the shank 1¼in (32mm) below the top and carefully wrap one turn of masking tape below your mark so that the tape sits squarely. The top edge of the tape is your cutting mark. With a hacksaw, make a cut following the line of the tape right the way round

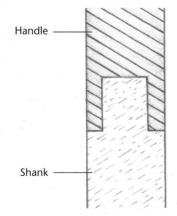

Handle ——

Shank ——

Fig 5.15 *My preferred method of shanking wood to wood.*

Fig 5.16 *To make a dowel, cut right round the shank . . .*

Fig 5.17 *. . . open up a small groove with a sharp knife . . .*

Fig 5.18 *. . . then rasp round the shank to form a dowel of the desired diameter.*

the shank, to a depth of approximately ¼in (6mm) (*see* Fig 5.16). Remove the tape. Use a sharp knife to open a small groove above the saw cut (*see* Fig 5.17), and then carefully rasp round the shank down to this cut, until you have formed a dowel of approximately ½in (13mm) diameter (*see* Fig 5.18).

Next, mark the centre of the handle and, with a ½in (13mm) wood bit, carefully drill a hole 1¼in (32mm) deep (*see* Fig 5.19). Try the handle for fit and clean up the dowel until you are satisfied with the quality of the joint. You will find it helpful if, using a sharp knife, you scrape round the hole in the handle to produce a shallow dish (*see* Fig 5.20). This will allow the shoulder of the dowel to fit tightly up to the handle at the joint.

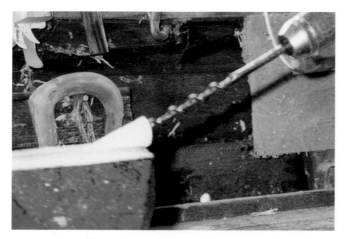

Fig 5.19 *Drill a hole in the centre of the base of the handle to take the dowel.*

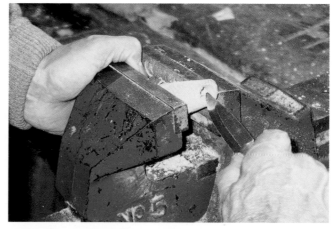

Fig 5.20 *Scrape round the hole in the handle to produce a shallow dish: this will give a tight fit.*

When you are satisfied, use an epoxy resin glue, sparingly, to fix the handle to the shank. Be careful not to split the handle by forcing the shank into it. Immediately remove any surplus glue squeezed out at the joint, and hold the joint in place until the glue sets. I have found that the best way to do this is by clamping the shank horizontally in a vice (making sure that the bark is suitably protected), placing an elastic expander strap over the handle and then hooking this on to the vice overnight (*see* Fig 5.21).

REFINING THE HANDLE

It is now time to return to the handle and finish sanding it so that it is of exactly the same diameter as the shank at the joint. Since this process involves sanding the handle right up to where it meets the bark (which can be easily damaged), I recommend that you protect the shank with a single turn of masking tape (*see* Fig 5.22). When you gain confidence and expertise you can omit this safeguard, but for the time being it is a useful protective measure.

Sand the handle in line with the grain, using increasingly fine grades of abrasive paper until all marks are removed and you are satisfied with the finish of both the handle and the joint. Remove the masking tape and, *very carefully*, finish sanding the handle so that when you rub your thumb over the joint it feels smooth.

FINISHING

To finish the stick, reduce the length of the shank if necessary, then fit a ferrule, clean, and varnish.

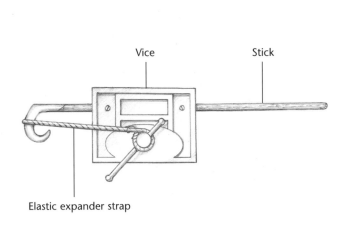

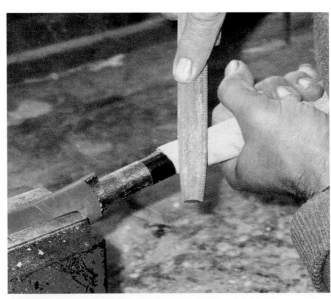

Fig 5.21 *Hold the handle and shank together securely whilst the glue sets.*

Fig 5.22 *A turn of masking tape will protect the shank from scratches as you rasp the handle.*

A TWO-PIECE WOODEN CROOK

The first thing to say about a crook made this way is that no matter how the handle is formed it will not, without some form of reinforcement, stand up to the task for which it was originally designed, i.e. restraining a struggling ewe. That said, a well-finished crook with a distinctive handle is a joy to hold and a pleasure to use.

The one I am going to describe, based on the pattern shown in Fig 5.23, will have a handle made from burr elm and a shank made from a nicely marked piece of hazel, about 48in (1,200mm) long.

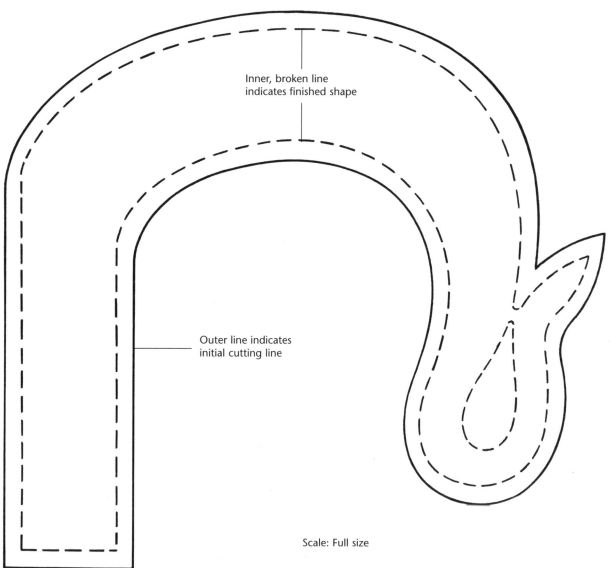

Inner, broken line indicates finished shape

Outer line indicates initial cutting line

Scale: Full size

Fig 5.23 *Template for crook handle.*

A burr is a distortion of the natural growth on a tree and, as can be seen from Fig 5.24, usually takes the form of a large, rounded lump similar in appearance to a fungal growth. Because the grain of the wood inside a burr is contorted, when a section is cut from it, that piece will contain the most attractive grain patterns, including whorls and bird's-eye effects (*see* Fig 5.25). A handle cut from a burr will also be stronger than one cut from a normal piece of wood because the grain, which does not run in the same direction, is less prone to weak spots.

Fig 5.24 *The distorted growth of a burr produces attractive grain patterns.*

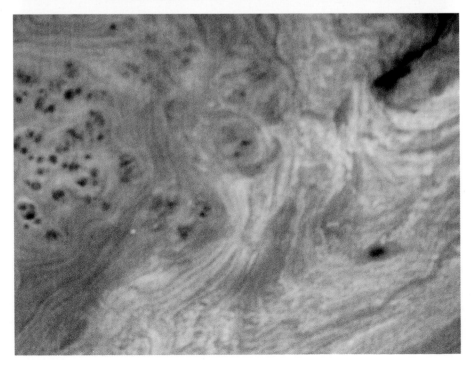

Fig 5.25 *Whorls and bird's eye patterns of burr grain.*

The piece of burr I am going to use is one I obtained from a local wood mill some years ago when large numbers of trees were devastated by gale force winds. The block is approximately 7 x 7 x 1¼in (178 x 178 x 32mm).

The processes involved in making a crook are essentially the same as those for making a market stick. We start, therefore, by transferring the pattern shown in Fig 5.23 on to a piece of Perspex or similar, and cutting out a template.

You will notice that the shape of this crook handle differs from that used to produce the one-piece crook. I have done this not only for the sake of variety, but also to help develop hand skills through carving the loop at the nose – a basic design into which a number of variations can be introduced. You should also notice another two of the relationships mentioned earlier in this chapter (*see* page 47). First, the nose of a crook handle should always be set approximately ½in (13mm) above its joint with the shank, and second, whilst the inside line of the neck should follow that of the shank, the outside line should lean back a little: a deviation of around ⅛in (3mm) between the top and bottom of a 4in (102mm) neck is about right.

SHAPING THE HANDLE

When the template has been cut, position it on the burr and move it around until it incorporates the most attractive patterns. Mark round the template in pencil and cut out the handle outline. To form the loop at the nose, drill two ⁵⁄₃₂in (4mm) holes – one close to the top line of the loop, the other near the bottom line – then use a coping saw to carefully remove the pear-shaped waste piece.

FITTING HANDLE TO SHANK

As before, use a power file or series of rasps to round over the square surfaces of the handle until you have achieved a satisfactory cylindrical shape, tapering towards the nose.

When you have brought the neck of the handle to a diameter of about ⅛in (3mm) larger than the shank you have selected, drill a ½in (13mm) central hole, 1¼in (32mm) deep, into the end of the handle to take the shank dowel.

This dowel should be made in exactly the same way as that of the market stick, except that this time we are going to strengthen it by incorporating a 4in (102mm) nail. When you have produced the dowel and are satisfied with the way it fits into the handle socket, cut the head off a 4in (102mm) nail and then carefully drill a ³⁄₁₆in (5mm) central hole into the dowel to take the entire length of the nail (*see* Fig 5.26).

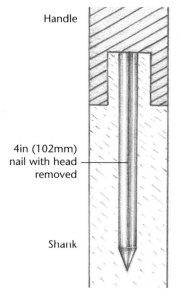

Handle

4in (102mm) nail with head removed

Shank

Fig 5.26 *Inserting a nail will give extra strength to a dowel joint.*

This reinforcement will help to prevent the shank fracturing below the handle joint when in use – particularly by over-enthusiastic sheep dog trialists as they bang the ground in an attempt to get a stubborn ewe into the final pen!

FINISHING

The handle should be shanked and brought to its final finish as with the market stick. Only when varnish is applied will the particular beauty of the burr handle become evident. To enhance it even further, when the last coat of varnish has properly dried, I like to cut it back very lightly with 0000 grade wire wool dipped in beeswax polish. It can then be rubbed with a dry cloth to produce a wonderful sheen, as is evident in the finished crook.

STRENGTHENING HANDLES

As a footnote to this section, I would like to return to an issue I raised earlier concerning the weak points which could develop in a handle cut from a straight-grained piece of wood. In order to reduce the risk of breaks occurring where short grain is in evidence, it is possible, and perfectly acceptable, to introduce some form of reinforcement at these points. I have used two methods with good results.

METHOD 1

The first method involves drilling a ³⁄₁₆in (5mm) hole across the entire length of the handle and inserting a piece of hardwood dowel of the type readily available at most DIY stores. The hole is best drilled using a stand-mounted electric drill, immediately after the handle shape has been cut. It is far easier to keep the hole in line when you are dealing with square edges to the handle than it is after they have been rounded off. The dowel should be cut to the full length of the hole, sparingly coated with epoxy wood glue and gently pushed in to fill the hole. Once the glue has set, the handle can be worked in the normal way. (*See* Fig 5.27.)

Of course, the dowel will show up, particularly when the handle is of darker wood, in which case it can either be left as a feature or stained to match the handle. Another method of camouflage is to cut the dowel an inch (25mm) short of the length of the hole in order to leave a ¹⁄₂in (13mm) gap at either end of the hole. Both of these gaps can then be filled with plugs cut from the same piece of wood as the handle. If these are cut with a plug cutter in a mounted drill, from a piece with similar grain, and glued in place so that the grain matches, they will be even less intrusive in the finished handle.

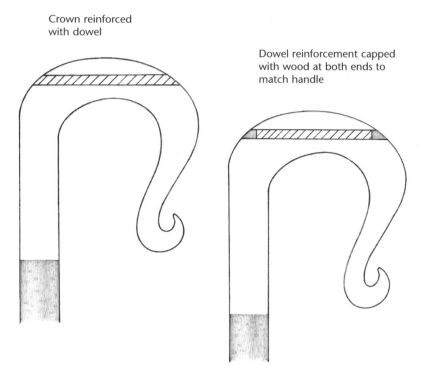

Crown reinforced
with dowel

Dowel reinforcement capped
with wood at both ends to
match handle

Fig 5.27 *Methods of strengthening handles with hardwood dowel.*

METHOD 2

The second method of reinforcement involves cutting through the length of the handle at the crown and inserting a plastic fillet formed from an offcut of Formica or similar material. The cut should be made with a tenon saw whilst the handle is still in, or close to, its squared-off state. The saw should be taken right through the length and thickness of the handle, making sure that the line of the cut is parallel to the sides of the handle at all times (*see* Fig 5.28); if it wanders, the final effect will be spoiled.

Fig 5.28 *Cutting through the length of the handle to insert a plastic fillet.*

Having completed the cut, the plastic piece should be positioned in the slot and a pencil used to mark on it the outline of the handle (*see* Fig 5.29). The plastic should then be removed and the outline cut carefully to avoid the edges chipping, after which it can be glued in place and left to set. Once set, the handle can be shaped as usual.

When finished, the insert will show up as a not unpleasing straight dark line, assuming the handle is of a light-coloured wood. If the handle is of darker wood, it will be difficult to distinguish.

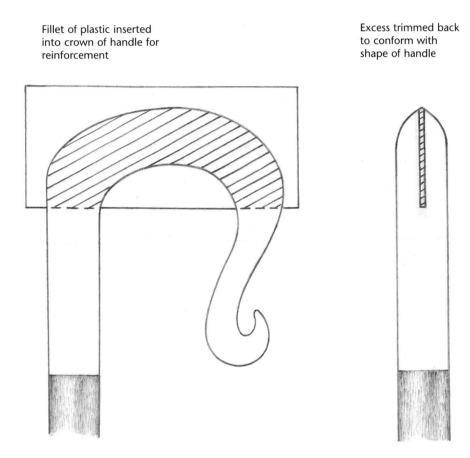

Fillet of plastic inserted into crown of handle for reinforcement

Excess trimmed back to conform with shape of handle

Fig 5.29 *Trimming the plastic fillet to fit the handle.*

CHAPTER SIX

RAM'S HORN AND ANTLER WALKING STICKS

So far, our efforts have concentrated on producing all-wood sticks. It is now time to consider the attractions of alternative materials. I'm going to describe how to use two of these, ram's horn and deer antler, to make good quality walking sticks. Before starting work with these materials it is important to understand some of their properties.

PROPERTIES OF RAM'S HORN

Let's look first at ram's horn. In the rough, ram's horn appears to be a solid, rigid, bone-like substance not dissimilar to antler. But in reality the two are quite different. Whereas antler is bone, ram's horn has more in common with a fingernail. It contains a central core or quick which may extend in a taper for up to one-third of the internal length of the horn. Whilst this quick is easily removed in one piece by drying the horn for a month or so and then giving it a sharp tap against the edge of a work bench, it leaves behind a substantial cavity (*see* Fig 6.1). Much of the horn shell which is left will have to be discarded, particularly if it has come from a young ram, when the thickness of the shell at its base may be less than 1/8in (3mm). In older rams the shell may be three times as thick and, ideally, this is the quality of horn we are looking for to make sticks – particularly full-size crooks.

Two-piece Cardigan stick. Hazel shank and handle made from black (Welsh mountain) ram's horn.

Fig 6.1 *Ram's horn has a 'rounded, triangular' shape, and a large central quick which leaves a hollow when removed.*

Another distinguishing property of ram's horn is that it is relatively easy to bend and shape after it has been heated, while antler, because it is bone, cannot be bent and can only be shaped by filing or cutting.

If you look at the ram's horn in Fig 6.1, you will see that the end section resembles a rounded triangle. To bring this to a more workable shape the horn needs to be squeezed, after heating, into a more circular cross section. This process, known as 'bulking', also helps to close the diameter of the cavity at the base of the horn, which in most cases is the end which will provide the point of attachment to the shank. However, the first stick we are going to make will be shanked at the other end (i.e. close to its tip).

A CARDIGAN STICK IN RAM'S HORN

The shape of this stick will already be familiar from Chapter 4. To produce it we require the use of two different pairs of moulds or formers: these must be made or bought before work on the stick begins.

ESSENTIAL EQUIPMENT

The first pair of formers will be used to bring the horn close to the handle shape we are seeking. They can be made from hard wood or metal to the dimensions shown in Fig 6.2. If you decide to make these, it is important to note that in the bottom former the rounded corners are *not* exactly the same shape. One has had less of the corner removed to accommodate the neck (or shank) end of the horn; the other, which is much more rounded, will take the nose end.

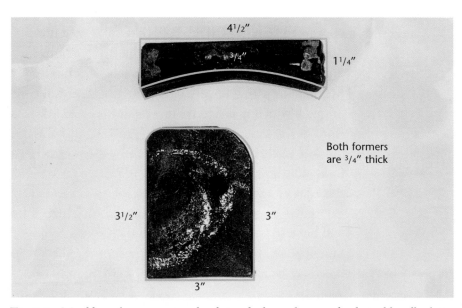

Fig 6.2 *Moulds or formers are used to bring the horn closer to the desired handle shape.*

The second pair of formers, which will be used to squeeze (i.e. bulk) the horn to make the neck of the handle, can be made from a 3in (76mm) length of 1¼in (32mm) diameter metal pipe, sawn lengthways into two equal pieces (*see* Fig 6.3). To reinforce these pieces, I have welded a short section of steel sheet to the back of each; whilst this is not critical it does make them easier to handle in the vice and also helps to prevent the pieces of pipe from splaying outwards when under pressure.

In both cases, the moulds I have described are not difficult or costly to make, but if you prefer to purchase something ready-made and more sophisticated, then the suppliers listed (*see* page 144) will be able to help. In addition to these moulds, you will also need an engineers' vice, a 7 x 7in (178 x 178mm) metal plate, ¼in (6mm) thick, a 7in (178mm) G-cramp and two 5in (127mm) G-cramps in order to exert and sustain the pressure needed to shape the horn until it has set. The sizes for the G-cramps are minimum sizes and are not critical.

Fig 6.3 *Formers used for bulking, made from a metal pipe sawn in half.*

SUITABLE HORN

When you have acquired this equipment, you next have to acquire a suitable horn. No longer the simple task it once was, unless you know someone who can provide one for you, the suppliers listed (*see* page 144) will be your best source. Good horn is not easy to come by and is not cheap. The type we require for this stick need not be of premium crook-making quality, nor does it need to be of substantial dimensions. The initial length should be about 15in (381mm) from base to tip and around 2¼in (55mm) in diameter at the base, which should have a shell wall no less than ⅛in (3mm) thick. All horns have a concave side which will be more pronounced in some and less in others (*see* Fig 6.4). Always look for horns which are at the lesser end of this scale – removing the concave shape can be difficult, particularly for beginners!

Fig 6.4 *All horns have a concave side.*

Fig 6.5 *The quick should loosen and come out as one piece with a gentle tap.*

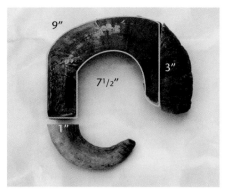

Fig 6.6 *This reassembled horn shows where the cuts are made to reveal the workable section for the handle.*

Fig 6.7 *The workable section for the handle in its initial state.*

Having acquired the horn, check whether the quick is still in place. If it is, tap the base of the horn gently but firmly on a solid surface and the quick should loosen and come out as one piece (*see* Fig 6.5). If it doesn't loosen after four or five taps, leave it to dry further, but don't be tempted to hasten the process by drying it in the oven as this may cause the horn to distort and split!

CUTTING THE HORN TO LENGTH

After removing the quick, keep it to one side: do not discard it as it may be of use later on. We can now prepare to cut the horn to an approximate length of 9in (229mm), taken from the best section of the horn. Whilst this has to be a matter of judgement, what we are attempting to produce is a piece which will be as solid as possible and which, after cutting the tip off, will produce sufficient material to bulk into a diameter of no less than 1in (25mm) to form the neck of the handle (*see* Fig 6.7).

Before making your first cut at the tip end, mark the horn at the point where you judge it will provide an adequate diameter and then measure off 9in (229mm) towards the base to ensure that you have enough material to play with. In Fig 6.6, the reassembled sections show where I made my cuts and Fig 6.7 shows what the workable section of handle looks like in its initial state.

HEATING TO REMOVE THE CURL

The next step is to heat the horn in order to make it supple before starting to bring it into shape by straightening out any remaining curl in the horn. The simplest means of heating it is to boil it in an old saucepan for about 30 minutes. The heat source could be the kitchen range so long as you, or others, do not object to the unusual smell!

When it's done, remove it from the saucepan with a suitable utensil – I use a pair of barbecue tongs, which are ideal – and let the hot water drain off for a moment. The horn will, of course, be hot, but not to the extent that it will burn you. Nevertheless, test it by picking it up carefully so that you are satisfied that it is not too hot for you to handle comfortably. Quickly transfer it to the metal plate and clamp it with the two 5in (127mm) G-cramps, tightening them until the curl is flattened out. Leave it to cool and set overnight.

SHAPING THE HANDLE

When the horn is removed from the cramps it has to be reheated in order to start bending it into the approximate handle shape. If we were to repeat the boiling water method we would run the risk of the horn resuming its original shape – complete with curl! So this time we are going to use dry heat, generated by a hot air gun of the paint stripper variety. Whilst some stickmakers use, and recommend, a blow torch for this job, I do not. The naked flame it produces is more likely to scorch the surface of the horn, and it is also inherently dangerous.

Place the horn between the top and bottom formers and use the vice to exert sufficient pressure to keep it in place. Play the hot air gun, carefully, along and around the crown of the handle and after 3–4 minutes try tightening the vice a little. The horn should give and start to assume the shape of the formers. Continue heating and tightening until it does, but do not force it. If the temperature is right it will give way readily without excessive pressure being required.

As the formers close up on the horn, fix the 7in (178mm) G-cramp in place and start to tighten that, too, so that all-round pressure is being exerted (*see* Fig 6.8). Take care at this stage to avoid any tendency for the horn to twist out of line. Should it start to do so, you may need to apply another G-cramp to restrain it at that point.

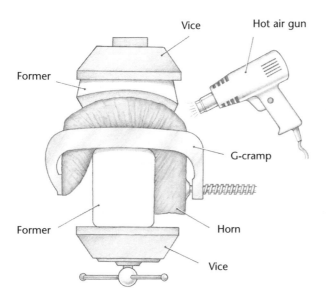

Fig 6.8 Shaping the handle using formers for shape, a hot air gun for dry heat, and a vice and G-cramp for pressure.

When the horn follows the shape of the formers for the whole of its length, you may withdraw the heat and stop tightening the vice. Leave it in the vice overnight to cool and set.

FORMING THE NECK

Bulking the neck of the handle is the next process and we shall need the hot air gun for this too. Before positioning the moulds made from the cut pipe, rasp down any high spots on the neck of the horn so that the diameter is approximately equal throughout the 3in (76mm) section we are going to squeeze. When you have done this, place the formers around the neck and set them in the vice, tightening the jaws so that the horn is gripped securely (*see* Fig 6.9). Using the same principles as before, heat and squeeze the horn until the formers have closed up or are prevented from doing so by horn which has been extruded in the process. Don't worry if a welt of horn appears between the jaws of the formers: this can easily be removed later – do not attempt to do so now.

Leave the handle to cool in the vice overnight then remove the pipe formers. The handle should now look like that shown in Fig 6.10. You can see from this that it is starting to look something like a Cardigan shape.

Fig 6.9 The neck is formed by gripping the horn (placed in formers) in the vice, and applying heat and pressure.

Fig 6.10 The shape of the handle after the neck has been formed.

FILLING THE CAVITY

Before continuing the shaping process, I want to turn our attention to the cavity which still remains in the handle. Unless this is filled, the finished handle will always have a fragile feel to it and will run the risk of cracking under everyday use, so it has to be filled. The easiest and most effective way of doing so, I have found, is by pouring liquid resin into the cavity. I use Isopon, but there are several brands available. If the cavity is a large one, I economize by replacing part of the horn quick, which we put aside earlier, as 'ballast'. Set the horn lightly in the vice, mix the resin with its hardener and pour in the liquid so that it reaches the brim. Leave to harden. We can then proceed to bring the handle to its final shape.

SMOOTHING THE HANDLE

To smooth the handle and refine its shape, use rasps and abrasive paper in exactly the same way as we did with the wooden Cardigan stick in Chapter 4 (*see* page 41), but remember two things:

1 The characteristics of horn are quite different from those of wood. Whilst it is easy to work, it is also easy to mark; without care some marks may prove indelible.
2 Horn is not solid. If you remove too much of its outer surface you risk exposing the cavity area. So the watchword is *care*!

Shape the handle to the profile shown in Fig 4.1, gradually and patiently. Remove it from the vice regularly and consider the shape from all angles as it develops. Do not take too much from one side before turning your attention to the opposite side: keep both sides in balance as you continue to remove surplus horn.

Occasionally, you may expose a surface flaw in the horn which couldn't be foreseen in its original state. If this cannot be taken out by careful sanding, it can usually be filled in with a mixture of glue and the filings from the horn. When dry, this filler can be sanded to the point where it becomes unobtrusive.

CAPPING THE OPEN END

Once you are satisfied with the final shape of the handle, the end which contained the cavity needs to be capped off. To make the cap we need to slice a disc about 1/8in (3mm) thick and with a diameter slightly larger than the end of the handle, lengthways from the base of a horn. For this stick I have used a piece of buffalo horn from an offcut produced in the manufacture of the market stick and crook described in Chapter 7, but ram's horn or cow horn will do equally well. If suitable pieces cannot be obtained from materials already in your possession, they can be purchased cheaply from the suppliers listed (*see* page 144). Cut the disc to the shape of the cavity end of the handle, making it slightly oversize in the process – 1/8in (3mm) all round will be ample.

Place the disc against the cavity and position it so that any pattern lines up with that of the handle (*see* Fig 6.11). Run a pencil around the circumference of the handle so that the shape is transferred to the back of the disc. This line will help to position it exactly when it is being glued. Apply epoxy glue to the back of the disc and position it on the handle. To keep it under pressure whilst the glue sets, put it in the vice and tighten gently.

When it has set, sand down the disc, using fine abrasive paper wrapped round a straight edge, until it exactly conforms to the profile of

Fig 6.11 *Positioning the material for the handle's cap: align any patterns on the cap material with any that appear on the handle.*

the end of the handle. A thin cap provides a better looking finish than a thick one, so reduce the thickness of the horn disc by sanding down from the original ⅛in (3mm) to something like ¹⁄₁₆in (1.5mm). Its edges, where they meet the handle, should be finely sanded and slightly rounded over. What we are aiming to achieve is an impression that the handle is a solid entity with the cap merging seamlessly into it. The handle is now ready to be fitted to the shank.

FIXING HANDLE TO SHANK

Instead of using a dowel to shank this stick, I'm going to introduce another method which many stickmakers prefer because it allows a little more room for manoeuvre and, arguably, it also makes for a stronger joint. It involves inserting a metal rod first into the diameter of the handle at the neck, and then into the shank (*see* Fig 6.12). This system of fixing may have evolved from the original practice of using a dowel screw, which has a thread at both ends, to fix ornate knob handles to fancy canes. Such a device might have stood the test of use by a Victorian 'toff', but it will certainly not cope with the rigours of a hill walk!

Although I have seen a 6in (152mm) nail with the head removed substituted for the dowel screw, the mild steel of the nail and its inadequate diameter do not provide sufficient strength.

The most acceptable material from which to manufacture a joining rod is that known as engineers' studding. This is a threaded rod which comes in varying diameters and is available in 1m lengths which can readily be cut to size. The diameter used for shanking this type of stick is ³⁄₁₆in (5mm).

To fit the rod, first cut off a piece which is sufficient to penetrate about three-quarters of the length of the handle neck and about 2in (51mm) into the shank. For the stick we are making, a piece 4in (102mm) long will do. Set the handle in a vice with the diameter of the neck uppermost and, with an electric drill, make a ³⁄₁₆in (5mm) central hole to a depth of around 1¾in (44mm). Because the depth of the hole will vary according to the length of the neck, be very careful not to drill too deeply. As a guide you will find it helpful to wrap a turn of adhesive tape around the drill bit at a distance no greater than the maximum depth of hole desired. Clean out the hole and try the rod for fit. If satisfied, set the rod in place by coating it with epoxy glue and pushing home gently. Immediately wipe off any surplus glue as it will be difficult to remove later and could interfere with the joint. The handle should look like Fig 6.13. When the glue has set, it can be fitted to the shank.

The shank is a piece of hazel 33in (838mm) long with a diameter at the top of ⅞in (22mm), and attractive bark which will complement the polished horn of the finished handle.

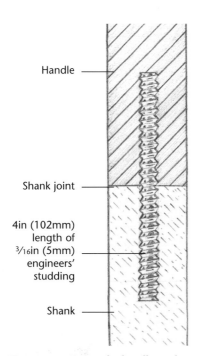

Handle

Shank joint

4in (102mm) length of ³⁄₁₆in (5mm) engineers' studding

Shank

Fig 6.12 *Fixing the handle to the shank with a metal rod.*

Fig 6.13 *The handle with the metal rod fixed in place.*

Set the shank in the vice, remembering to protect the bark, and as we did with the handle, drill a ³⁄₁₆in (5mm) diameter central hole to a depth which equals the length of rod protruding from the handle. Avoid overdrilling the depth if you can, making sure that the hole is just deep enough to take the rod. Try it for fit (*see* Fig 6.14) and make good any imperfections in the joint with similar techniques to those we used to produce the two-piece wooden sticks in Chapter 5.

When you are satisfied with the quality of the joint, the diameter of the handle needs to be finished to match exactly that of the shank. Use fine abrasive paper for this, remembering to rub carefully with the grain of the handle and to avoid scuffing the bark of the shank. If you have any doubts, it takes only seconds to put a turn of protective tape in place on the shank, and this could save considerable heartache later.

Before gluing the handle into the shank, make a final check on how they sit together; this will be your last opportunity to make any alterations. Apart from the tightness of the joint and the exactness of diameter, does the handle follow the line of the shank? If you need to, you can tweak the joining rod in the vice to adjust the line a little – but don't overdo it. Take your time and get it right!

When you think it is right, coat the rod sparingly with epoxy glue and push it gently into the shank. Clean off any excess glue immediately and leave to dry in the vice under tension, as described earlier.

FINISHING

Fit a ferrule in the usual way and clean the shank of the stick. At this stage I recommend that you rub down the horn handle with a cloth dipped in T-CUT, Brasso or similar, or alternatively, liquid kitchen scourer. These contain fine abrasive particles in suspension and, carefully applied, will remove any remaining scratches in the horn. Dry off the handle prior to applying a protective finish.

There is some dispute amongst stickmakers (and judges of stickmaking competitions) as to whether varnish should ever be applied to horn. Traditionalists will argue that if any finish is applied, it should be of the oil or wax variety. What I will say is that varnish, properly applied, with the final coat being cut back lightly with 0000 grade wire wool dipped in beeswax polish, will look, and feel, as good as any finish.

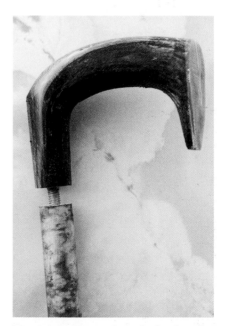

Fig 6.14 *Trying the rod, shank and handle for fit.*

FINISHES

If you want to experiment with other finishes, go ahead. Try using boiled linseed oil (which, incidentally, is bought ready-boiled). Applied with a cloth and burnished to a dull shine, it does look very attractive. Any stick finished in this way needs regular and continual oiling if it is to sustain its initial glow. An old saying has it that a new stick should be oiled:

> every day for a week
> once a week for a month
> every month for a year
> and once a year for life!

Another alternative is clear, solid beeswax as is used to seal cut wood. Apply it sparingly with a clean cloth and immediately polish to a sheen. Like oil, a wax finish needs to be refreshed regularly.

Do not be afraid to experiment with finishes. With experience, *you* will decide what suits you best, and that's the most important consideration. The completed example on page 61 has been varnished.

PROPERTIES OF ANTLER

When an antler is shed naturally, the point at which it was attached to the head, properly described as the coronet, remains intact and can be used as an attractive feature on any handle. Occasionally, a small protruberance of bone is attached to the base of the coronet and this is even better as it provides the opportunity to carve a figure or emblem from it. This is what I've done in the example shown in Fig 6.15.

To obtain red deer antler is not difficult since, in addition to substantial wild herds in England and Scotland, this species is commercially farmed throughout the country. If you cannot find a local source of supply, it will be available from the suppliers listed (*see* page 144). However, it is important when purchasing antler unseen, that you specify the type of stick you intend to make from it. You might otherwise end up with something which, though certainly antler, is totally unsuited to the project you had in mind.

Some antlers are far too bulky for practical purposes even though they might appear, initially, to offer attractive configurations. Remember that antler is bone and because of that it cannot be bent. In addition, it has a core of relatively soft porous material called pith. This runs through both the main stem and its offshoots (called tines) and rises quite close to the surface. If, therefore, you attempt to reduce the diameter of an oversize stem or tine by filing, you will very quickly expose the pith and spoil the product.

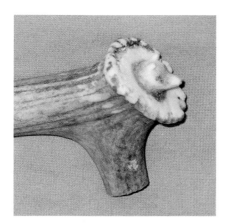

Fig 6.15 *An example of a figure carved in a bone protruberance from an antler.*

A CROSS-HEAD STICK IN ANTLER

In Great Britain the majority of antler are from one of four deer species – red, fallow, roe and sika (left to right in Fig 6.16). Red is the most common and sika the least. All deer shed, or cast, their antlers each year and these provide suitable materials for making a variety of sticks.

From Fig 6.16 it is evident that some antlers offer greater potential and versatility than others. The small antlers of a roe deer, for example, are only likely to produce thumbstick handles whilst those of a red deer can be used for thumbsticks, upright handles and 90° handles of the type I am going to describe.

ADAPTING YOUR MATERIAL

For the stick I am going to make, we need a piece of red deer antler which incorporates the coronet and includes a right angle from which the handle and neck of the stick will be formed. The handle section needs to be a minimum of 6in (152mm) long with a diameter of around 1in (25mm). Ideally, the neck piece coming off it at the right angle should be a minimum of 1½in (38mm) long, with the same diameter as the head. However, as we are dealing with nature, we cannot simply order a piece to fit our ideal dimensions. We have to make the best of what is available, and that is what I have done with the example shown in Fig 6.17.

In this case the tine section which formed the neck of the stick, and to which the shank was attached, was narrower than I would have liked. If I had attempted to fit a shank straight on to it as it originally stood, the shank would have needed to match and, in consequence, would have been much too slender for any sort of practical use. The handle would also have looked top heavy in comparison with the shank. The ploy I

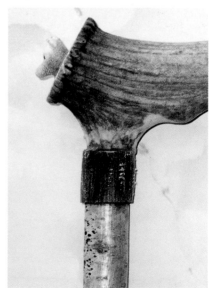

Fig 6.17 A collar has been added to the join of shank and handle to disguise the differences in diameter.

Fig 6.16 Antlers from different species of deer. Left to right: red, fallow, roe, sika.

have used, to allow me the choice of a more substantial shank, is to fit a collar at the point where the handle is joined to the shank. This effectively disguises the difference in the respective diameters of the neck and shank and, at the same time, adds strength to the joint. I will describe how to make and fit this type of collar later. First we need to cut the handle to length.

CUTTING AND DECORATING

Measure $5\frac{1}{2}$in (140mm) from the base of the coronet and use a hacksaw to make a straight cut through the diameter of the section you have decided will form the handle piece. You will, in the process, expose the pith – I will explain how to disguise this.

Before proceeding to fit the handle to the shank, now is the time to introduce any embellishment to the coronet end of the handle. This can vary according to your ambition and your skill with pen and carving knife. For example, if the antler you have acquired has a coronet which has a fairly level surface already, use fine abrasive paper to bring it to a smooth dome. You may then paint, with acrylic paints, whatever takes your fancy – your initials, an animal's head, an emblem or crest.

For a variation on this theme you could produce a scrimshaw effect. Use a pencil to draw in, for example, a deer's head, scratch around the pencil guideline with a sewing needle, rub some colouring agent (such as black shoe polish) into the scratched outline, immediately removing any excess, and gently buff with very fine sandpaper to finish.

Another alternative is to drill out a shallow hole to accommodate exactly a small coin or medallion which could be set carefully in place with epoxy glue. Or, you could drill deeper into the coronet in order to inset, say, a small fishing-fly as a feature. To achieve this effect you would need, after drilling an appropriately sized hole, to seal any exposed pith with white paint or filler. Then, pour in some clear liquid resin, of the kind used to make paperweights, to half fill the hole and place in position whatever object you have chosen, before pouring more resin over it to fill the hole to the brim. Be careful not to overfill the hole as it is difficult to remove any surplus resin, and avoid introducing any bubbles by pouring slowly and consistently. Leave the handle until the resin has set properly and you will have produced an unusual and attractive effect.

CARVING THE HANDLE

Finally, perhaps the most difficult task, if the coronet retains a sufficient piece of bone attached to it, you might decide to introduce a small carving, as I have done in Fig 6.15. If there *is* sufficient material to work on then go ahead and try out your skill as a carver. On this scale, it's not as difficult as it might first appear and the beauty of it is, if you are

unhappy with the result you can always remove it and create one of the other features or leave it as a plain coronet.

If you do decide on a carving, I strongly recommend that you make a clay model, to finished size, of whatever it is you've chosen to feature. If you are not satisfied with the model, then it is very unlikely that you will be happy with any carving you attempt. If the model looks good, use a small craft knife and needle files to replicate its features in the bone of the coronet. To produce the collie, I started by roughly squaring off the irregular piece of bone to the overall size of the head I had decided upon, then I drew in some datum points – the centre of the ears, position of the eyes, location of the nose and mouth: nothing detailed, just enough to keep the shape of the head balanced – before proceeding to carve out the profile.

I always start with the highest points – the ears – and when I am satisfied with the shape and position of those I move forward to the forehead, eyes and nose. I then shape the underjaw, starting from the nose and moving backwards into the neck. I do not attempt to finish one area completely before moving on, as each section of the head has to be shaped in relation to the next until it starts to come together as a whole. The secret of any carving is not to take too much off in one go – patience and sharp tools are required. Keep referring back to the model and if you do slip up and lop off an ear or take too much off the nose, don't worry. It is usually quite easy to repair the mistake with a little plastic filler which, when painted, will be undetectable.

When you are satisfied with your efforts, go on to paint the head. I recommend using acrylic paints – they are easy to use and give a good depth of colour. I painted the collie's head white all over, before painting in the black markings and finally, using a pin, touching in the brown eyes. Always start by putting on the light colours before laying on the darker ones – it's much easier and more effective.

CAPPING OFF

To finish off the handle, we now need to turn our attention to its other end which, you will remember, still has the exposed pith in evidence. To tidy this up, we need to cap the end with a piece of attractive, contrasting material. I have seen various hardwoods used effectively, but I like to use a piece of solid ram's horn, usually an offcut from another stick I've made. The thickest part of the horn tip we cut off from the Cardigan stick would work well.

The cap we are going to produce will be shaped like a mushroom, the stem of which will fit snugly into a hole drilled into the end section of the handle (see Fig 6.18). The diameter of the mushroom cap will be determined by the diameter of the antler handle, the cap being cut slightly oversize to allow for final finishing when set in place.

Mushroom cap

Handle

Fig 6.18 *A mushroom cap is formed from an offcut of horn, cut, and shaped to fit the handle end.*

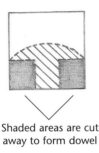

Cap is formed
from circular
plug of horn

Shaded areas are cut
away to form dowel

Fig 6.19 *Shaping the dowel of the mushroom cap.*

To start with, cut a plug ⁵⁄₈in (16mm) long from the widest end of the horn offcut and file it to the approximate circumference of the antler handle, leaving it ¹⁄₈in (3mm) oversize all the way round. The stem, or dowel, should then be shaped by measuring and carefully marking the circumference of the plug, ³⁄₈in (10mm) from one end. Using a small hacksaw follow the line of the mark, cutting to a depth of about ¹⁄₄in (6mm). Then, with a ¹⁄₂in (13mm) wood chisel, chip away the area shaded in Fig 6.19 and clean it up with a file and sandpaper to produce a circular dowel of ¹⁄₂in (13mm) diameter.

Next, drill a hole lengthways into the pith of the handle, ¹⁄₂in (13mm) in diameter and ³⁄₈in (10mm) in depth, and try the dowel of the plug for fit. Do not force it home as it has to come out again! If necessary, clean up the dowel and the shoulder of the plug until it fits tightly up to the end of the handle. Spend some time getting this part right. When you are satisfied, make a small pencil mark on the handle and a corresponding one on the plug so that you can realign them when they are glued. Remove the plug.

Before gluing it back in place, pour some liquid resin into the hole in the handle and let it soak into the pith. Top it up and leave it for a while until all of the resin in the hole has been absorbed. When dry, the resin will considerably strengthen the pith core.

Coat the dowel and base of the plug with epoxy glue, re-align the guide marks and push the plug into place. Keep it under pressure, with an elastic band or two stretched lengthways around the handle, until the glue sets. After this, file down the diameter of the plug until it corresponds exactly with the handle, and chamfer the edges to achieve a nicely rounded effect. To finish, smooth it off with fine abrasive paper.

FIXING HANDLE TO SHANK

The handle now needs to be set in the shank using the same steel pin method as for the horn Cardigan stick earlier in this Chapter. Because the antler neck offers much less material than the horn neck of the Cardigan stick, you will need to drill a shallower hole to take the pin this time. Take great care not to drill all the way through the handle! The pith surrounding the hole needs to be strengthened using the same principle as we used to cap the nose of the stick. Be sure that the pith absorbs as much resin as possible so that there is no risk of the pin subsequently working loose.

An alternative approach is to use a drill which is larger than the diameter of the pin in order to remove as much of the pith as possible without weakening the inside walls of the antler. The cavity should then be filled with resin and left to set. When hard, the resin core can be drilled to the same diameter as the pin, which should then be fixed in place with epoxy glue.

You will remember that I said we would incorporate a collar around the neck joint of this stick in order to disguise the difference between the diameters of the antler neck and the shank. The shank, incidentally, is made from hazel – on this occasion a pale shade with unusual 'snakeskin' mottling which complements the antler handle particularly well.

When you have set the pin in place in the handle and drilled the shank to take it, tidy the joint to ensure good contact between the base of the handle and the top of the shank.

MAKING A COLLAR

We now need to turn our attention to making the collar which, in essence, is a short tube which will cover the neck joint and disguise any discrepancies in it. Collars can be made from metal, bought ready-made in different sizes, or from hardwood, horn and antler. The difficulty with metal is that you have to make the stick fit the collar: the other materials can all be easily shaped to fit the stick. A presentation stick with an engraved silver collar can be most impressive, but that apart, the other materials are equally effective, and are certainly easier to work. For this collar I am going to use ram's horn.

To make the collar, first select an offcut piece of solid horn which has a diameter about ⅛in (3mm) larger than that of the shank if, as in this case, the shank diameter is larger than that of the handle. If the converse is true, then use the handle diameter as your guide. Cut a 1in (25mm) length from this offcut, making sure that the cuts at both ends are straight and parallel. This is important: any deficiencies now will spoil the effect later. Drill a central hole, ⅝in (16mm) in diameter, right through the plug to make the basic collar (see Fig 6.20).

The next stage is to fit the collar to the handle. To produce a neat, inset effect, we need to make a dowel at the base of the handle so that the collar, when finished, will butt up to it tightly and the thickness of the collar will be less evident (see Fig 6.21). As a guide for cutting, wrap

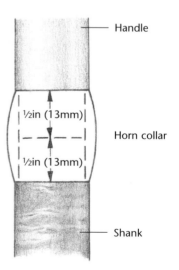

Ends of handle and shank dowelled slightly to allow collar to fit neatly

Fig 6.21 *Fitting the collar to the handle and shank.*

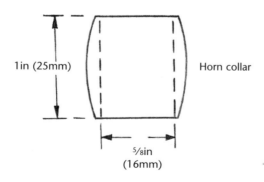

Fig 6.20 *Dimensions of horn collar.*

one turn of masking tape squarely round the base of the handle, at a distance equal to half the length of the collar. In this case, the collar is 1in (25mm) so the bottom edge of the tape is set back ½in (13mm). Using a small hacksaw, follow the line of the tape, making a cut about ⅛in (3mm) deep right round the neck of the handle. Remove the waste to form the dowel. Clean it up with abrasive paper and try the collar for fit. When satisfied, apply epoxy glue sparingly to the dowel and tap the collar into place (*see* Fig 6.22). Any surplus glue squeezed out should be wiped off immediately to prevent it marking the handle. When the glue has dried, repeat the process of making a dowel, this time on the top of the shank (*see* Fig 6.23). Fit the shank, glue and leave to set (*see* Fig 6.24).

What remains now is to shape the collar by rounding off any edges, initially with a needle rasp and then with fine abrasive paper. A turn of masking tape above and below the collar will help to prevent scratching either the shank or the handle. This should not be removed until the shaping process is complete.

Fig 6.22 *Tapping the collar into place on the handle.*

Fig 6.23 *Forming a dowel to fit the collar to the shank.*

Fig 6.24 *Fitting the shank to the collar and handle.*

FINISHING

To finish the stick, fit a ferrule and varnish the shank and collar as before. Whether you decide to varnish the antler handle or not is a personal choice. The considerations which apply to horn apply equally to antler. If you are unsure, try an oil or wax finish first. It is easier to replace either of these with varnish than it is the other way round. The finished stick, shown on page 71, has been varnished.

CHAPTER SEVEN

MARKET STICK AND CROOK IN BUFFALO HORN

WITH the increasing difficulty of acquiring supplies of good ram's horn, it is not really surprising that some enterprising stickmaker hit upon the idea of using buffalo horn as a substitute. It would be interesting to discover how this first came about, since buffalo horn of the type used in stickmaking has to come from Africa or the Far East. Who was it, I wonder, who originally identified the material as having the potential to make stick handles (which it has proved to have), and who imported the first supplies? Whoever it was has certainly contributed to the continuation of horn crook making in this country for today, supplies of buffalo horn are readily available here.

The animal which provides horn of this kind is a domesticated water buffalo, found in numbers in India, Burma, Thailand and Vietnam, although herds have also been introduced to Italy and Romania. I was interested to read recently that a small herd has been imported to a farm not 20 miles (34km) from where I live. How they will cope with the British climate remains to be seen!

Two-piece crook. The shank of unusual golden hazel is crowned with jet black buffalo horn.

PROPERTIES OF BUFFALO HORN

Buffalo horn comes in two varieties: black and coloured. The first is jet black, although occasionally it has grey or white streaks running through it below the surface. These streaks become apparent when the horn is worked and can provide attractive evidence that the material is a natural one and not synthetic as the pure black kind can suggest. The coloured variety is, I believe, softer than the black horn and easier to work. It certainly offers more interesting colour combinations of suffused greens, greys and browns. A crook I have just finished reminds me of the range of colours one sees on the plumage of a wild duck (*see* Fig 7.1).

Coloured horn is not as easy to come by as black and although it is generally available, you can expect to pay rather more for it.

Both varieties are dense and, therefore, relatively heavy. Because of its density, when we come to shape it we shall need to use the concentrated heat of a hot air gun.

When purchased in Britain, the horn comes as a solid piece with no inner core or cavities. This makes working it easier, since it avoids the need for bulking and infilling any hollows. There is a natural bend in the horn, but this works to our advantage. Unlike ram's horn, the bend remains in one plane and does not present the challenge of removing any curl.

CHOOSING YOUR MATERIAL

Figure 7.2 shows examples of buffalo horn as it would be purchased. You can see that it comes in a variety of lengths and base thicknesses. When buying horn, do not be fooled into believing that 'biggest is best': bigger pieces will certainly cost more and you may end up paying for a lot of waste material.

Buffalo horn is oval in section. For stickmaking purposes an area at the base of around 2¼ x 1¼in (57 x 32mm) will be needed. The length of horn required will vary according to the type of handle being made; for a market stick, 14in (356mm) will be sufficient, whilst a full-size crook will need 15–16in (381–406mm).

Fig 7.1 A fine example of coloured buffalo horn, showing attractive gradations in colour.

Fig 7.2 *Buffalo horn as it is bought.*

Fig 7.3 *My original home-made jig of hardwood and sash cramp.*

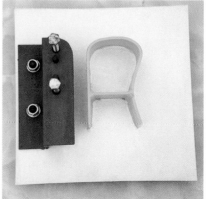

Fig 7.4 *A commercial bending jig.*

SHAPING THE HORN

To shape this type of horn requires not only concentrated dry heat, but also some means of pushing it into the desired shape and holding it there. When I started bending buffalo horn, I made a simple jig from a piece of hardwood and a sash cramp (*see* Fig 7.3). Whilst this is still a perfectly reasonable method, I have sought ways to improve on it and currently I use a bending jig of the type shown in Fig 7.4. Although relatively expensive to purchase, jigs of this type will last a lifetime and will certainly repay the investment if frequently used. They are obtainable from the suppliers listed (*see* page 144). Alternatively, something similar could be made by a competent metal worker. The attraction of a jig like this is its versatility, i.e. it can be used to shape any kind of horn and can be adjusted to accommodate 'nose-in' and 'nose-out' market sticks as well as full-size crooks. Figure 7.5 shows the four components of the bending jig:

1 a back plate (A);
2 a former, welded to the back plate and around which the handle will be bent (B);
3 an adjustable stay bolted to the back plate to allow the neck of the handle to be clamped tight up to the former (C); and
4 a bearer which rides within the stay and permits further adjustment to the clamping process (D).

Whatever method of bending and shaping you use, it is critical that your means of doing so are readily to hand before embarking on the production of a bent horn stick.

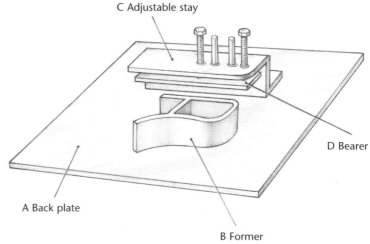

Fig 7.5 *The components of the bending jig.*

A BUFFALO HORN MARKET STICK

The simplest form of bent horn stick to produce is the 'nose-in' variety, similar in shape to the wooden version described in Chapter 5. Figure 5.1 (*see* page 44) shows the final shape and finished dimensions we are looking for in this market stick.

For extra embellishment, we are going to fit a short section of differently coloured horn (or antler) where the handle joins the shank. This insert, called a spacer, does not add to the strength of the joint in the same way as a collar. It is a purely decorative effect which highlights the quality of the joint and must therefore be a perfect fit. More on this shortly.

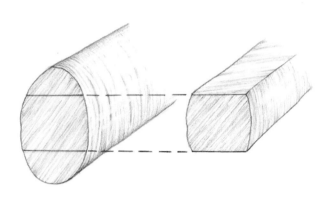

Fig 7.6 *Reducing the cross section of the buffalo horn to a roughly squared-off state.*

Fig 7.7 *The horn should be squared-off for as great a length as its shape and curve will allow.*

Fig 7.8 *When bending the horn, ensure that the surfaces of the horn are in all-round contact with the jig.*

Fig 7.9 *A G-cramp is used to ensure that the horn is in close contact with the former throughout the crown area.*

REDUCING THE HORN'S SIZE

To start with, we need to reduce the cross section of the buffalo horn in the area which will become the neck so that it will be easier to bend and less likely to wrinkle on the inside of the curve in the process.

Assuming that we are starting off with a horn which is a minimum of 14in (356mm) long, its oval base can be expected to be around 2in (51mm) in diameter at its widest point and 1in (25mm) at its narrowest. What we are aiming to do is reduce the widest point to approximately the same dimension as the narrowest so that the cross section at the base is roughly square (*see* Fig 7.6). We want to continue this square cross section as far up the horn as its shape and thickness will allow. It is impossible to give precise measurements for this part of the exercise, but Fig 7.7 gives some idea of what we are seeking to achieve initially. Using a coloured pencil or felt tip pen, sketch in this outline on the horn and then cut out the shape. A powered band saw is ideal for this purpose, but it is perfectly possible to obtain similar results with a coping saw or hacksaw. Be careful not to remove too much at this stage: we are not trying to achieve the final shape here, we are simply removing surplus material in order to facilitate subsequent shaping.

When you have finished cutting, use a file or rasp to tidy up the outline and round off any square edges.

HEATING AND BENDING

The next step is to boil the horn for about 30 minutes, which will soften it a little and help to speed up the process of bending with a hot air gun. Remember, when the horn is taken out of the boiling pot, it's going to be hot! As before, use a pair of tongs to extract it and test that it can be handled comfortably before moving it to whatever means of bending equipment you are about to use.

If it's a bending jig like the one I'm using in Fig 7.8, clamp the neck section between the adjustable stay and former and tighten down the bearer so that the surfaces of the horn are in all-round contact with the jig. Do not over-tighten the clamps; this is unnecessary and will only result in damage to the jig and/or the horn.

Before starting to heat the horn, squirt some lubricating oil along it to reduce the risk of scorching. Play the hot air gun for about five minutes along the section of horn which is going to be bent round the top of the former to become the crown of the handle. Use a G-cramp to force the horn around the former, tightening it until the horn is in close contact with the surfaces of the former throughout the area of the crown (*see* Fig 7.9). I also use roughly-shaped concave and convex wooden blocks and wedges to help this process (*see* Fig 7.10).

Fig 7.10 *Shaped wedges can help to keep the horn in contact with the former throughout the required length.*

Continue to heat the horn along its remaining length (i.e. the as yet unclamped section towards the tip) and use another G-cramp and a block to pull this section into line (*see* Fig 7.11). Do not, however, tighten these cramps to the extent that the horn is pulled right into the concave shape of the former. To make this a 'nose-in' stick, what we are aiming for at this stage is a shape which will be close to that shown in Fig 7.12.

Once all of the cramps are in place, check that the horn has not twisted away from the back plate of the jig. If it has, you will need to apply a further cramp or two to pull it back into alignment. When you are satisfied, leave the horn to set in the jig overnight.

The nose now needs to be turned in and this requires the area close to the tip – say the last 4in (102mm) or so – to be reheated and squeezed up in a vice. Wedge the handle as shown in Fig 7.13. Heat the nose end and tighten the vice gently until the nose starts to come round to a point about 2in (50mm) from the neck. Leave it in the vice to cool and set.

Fig 7.11 *To heat and bend the remaining tip of horn, an additional G-cramp and wooden block are required.*

Fig 7.12 *The shape to aim for after heating and bending.*

Fig 7.13 *Wedging the handle in order to turn the nose in.*

Fig 7.14 *Cutting the handle to length, with a hacksaw.*

CUTTING TO LENGTH

The finished length of the handle, from the point at which it joins the shank to the tip of its nose, should be about 12in (305mm). From Fig 5.1 (*see* page 44) you will also see that the nose is set slightly higher than the shank joint. This distance is not critical – indeed, I have seen acceptable sticks where the nose and joint were level with each other. What is not acceptable is to have the nose dipping lower than the shank joint. This appears to make the handle sag and would certainly be penalized by most judges of stickmaking competitions.

To allow for final trimming, measure a little more than 12in (305mm) from the shank end, mark, and cut with a hacksaw (*see* Fig 7.14).

FINAL SHAPING

What now remains is to bring the handle to its final shape and finish using a series of rasps and abrasive paper. The effect we are looking for is a nicely rounded handle which tapers at the nose to a blunt point.

Before you start, remember that this material works easily and it is much quicker to introduce unwanted marks than it is to remove them!

As far as you possibly can, file and sand along the length rather than around the circumference of the handle, and do not remove too much material from any one surface before moving to the next. Pause, assess, proceed should be the order of working.

Take particular care towards the tip – we are not looking to produce a point which appears to have come from a pencil sharpener! Figure 5.5 (*see* page 46) shows that the inner surface of the curve at the tip is flattened off somewhat, making the outer surface semicircular.

FIXING HANDLE TO SHANK

When you are happy with the shape and finish you have produced, it is time to fit the handle to the shank. We will do so using the metal rod method described in Chapter 6, but with the addition of a 'spacer' which will sit between handle and shank and decorate the joint. The spacer can be made from a variety of materials including:

- a hard wood, such as ebony
- antler or horn
- a metal, such as brass
- synthetic materials like nylon or tufnol.

I generally use horn – ram's horn to highlight a dark handle or buffalo horn when the handle is a lighter colour. Select a piece which has no evident flaws and which is sufficiently large in cross section to accommodate the circumference of the neck of the handle; the piece should be no more than ¾in (19mm) thick (*see* Fig 7.15).

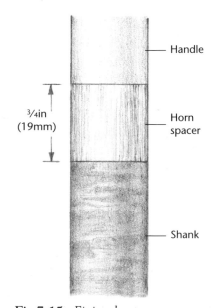

Fig 7.15 *Fitting the spacer.*

Handle

Horn spacer

Shank

¾in (19mm)

Fig 7.16 *Smoothing the top and bottom of the spacer to achieve level surfaces.*

The top and bottom surfaces of the piece need to be absolutely level, smooth and parallel with one another so that when the piece is fitted between handle and shank, it forms a perfect joint with both. The best way to achieve level surfaces, in my experience, is to rub the spacer on a piece of fine abrasive paper which is laid on a flat surface: this minimizes the risk of rounding over the edges (*see* Fig 7.16). When you are satisfied with these surfaces, proceed to remove most of the waste from the circumference of the spacer with a rasp, but do not, at this stage, attempt to bring it to finished dimensions. This will be done when it is fitted to the handle.

Next, drill the handle and fit an appropriate length of metal joining rod, on this occasion of ⅜in (10mm) diameter. Centre and drill the spacer to take the rod and slip the spacer in place on it. Adjust it to achieve the best fit and mark both the spacer and handle with a light scratch, to assist correct positioning on replacement. Remove the spacer, apply glue sparingly and replace it on the rod. To keep it in place and under tension, run a nut on to the rod and tighten it with finger pressure. Immediately wipe off any glue which has been squeezed out and when it has set, remove the nut.

Using abrasive paper, carefully rub down the spacer until its circumference exactly matches that of the handle.

Next, drill the shank out, try it for fit on the metal rod and, if necessary, further reduce the circumference of the spacer so that it marries up perfectly with the shank.

FINISHING

Finish the stick by fitting a ferrule and applying varnish, oil or polish.

A BUFFALO HORN CROOK

Many of the processes involved in producing a buffalo horn crook have already been described in the market stick project in this chapter. The main differences between the two lie in the overall dimensions and the shape of the handle. (*See* Fig 7.17 for the finished shape and final dimensions of this crook.) Both the shank and the handle of a crook will be larger than those of a market stick and whilst a market stick *can* have an out-turned nose, a crook should *always* have one. Producing this out turn is something we shall address later in this section.

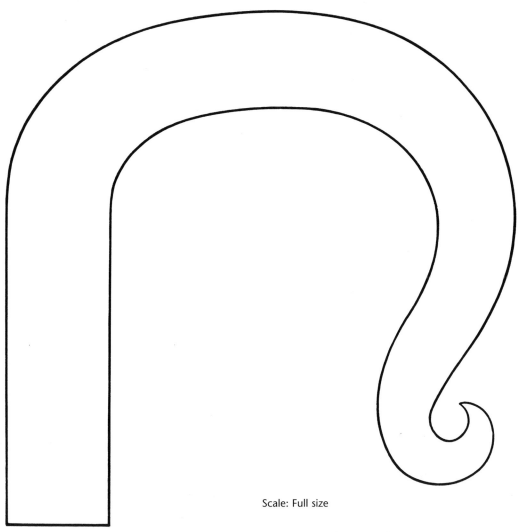

Scale: Full size

Fig 7.17 *Profile of finished buffalo horn crook.*

HEATING AND BENDING

To make a full-size crook we will need a horn between 15 and 16in (381 and 406mm) in length. As with the market stick, start by removing surplus horn, with a saw, from what will become the neck area to facilitate bending, then tidy up the saw cuts with a rasp.

Boil it for half an hour and transfer it quickly, but carefully, to the bending jig. Clamp the neck in place as before, then oil and heat the area which will become the crown of the handle with a hot air gun. Do this for five minutes. With G-cramps, pull the horn around the former ensuring that this time it follows the entire contour of the former, particularly the concave section, and clamp it firmly in place. I always complete this part of the process in one go, but if you are unsure at first, there is nothing to prevent you completing the bend around the crown and leaving this to set before moving on to shape the concave section. With experience you will find that the horn moves quite readily once it is up to heat, and the points at which you apply G-cramps, in order to keep the horn tight up to the former, will become self-evident as the horn starts to assume its shape.

When you are satisfied that the horn is in contact with the former throughout its length, and that it is securely clamped in place, leave it to set overnight. On removal from the jig it should look like the example shown in Fig 7.18.

At this stage, I like to tidy up the handle so that I can get a better feel for it as it is developing and so that I am not left with too much material to remove in the final stages. All that's needed is to rasp away any sharp edges and high points so that the circular shape of the handle and the line from the neck to the crown start to emerge. Remember what I said earlier: horn is easy to work, so be careful not to remove an excessive amount.

TURNING OUT THE NOSE

The next step is to turn out the nose of the handle. Before doing so, it is important to decide how much of a curl is required. This, in turn, will determine the nature of any additional equipment needed to produce it.

For example, if all you want is a modest turn like the one shown in Fig 7.19, then you will need very little extra equipment. Set the handle upside down in a vice, heat the area you wish to bend with a hot air gun and use grips to tweak it into the desired shape. Secure it with a cramp and leave it to set. When it has done so, use a hacksaw to remove any excess length, remembering that the nose needs to be set about 1/2in (13mm) higher than the base of the neck.

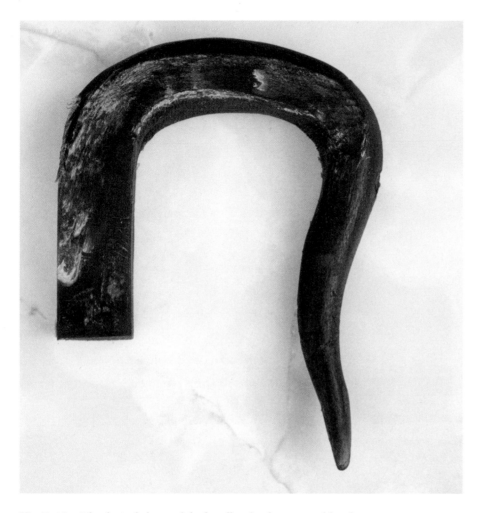

Fig 7.18 *The desired shape of the handle after heating and bending.*

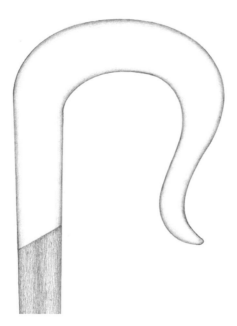

Fig 7.19 *Crook with half turned-out nose and angled shank joint.*

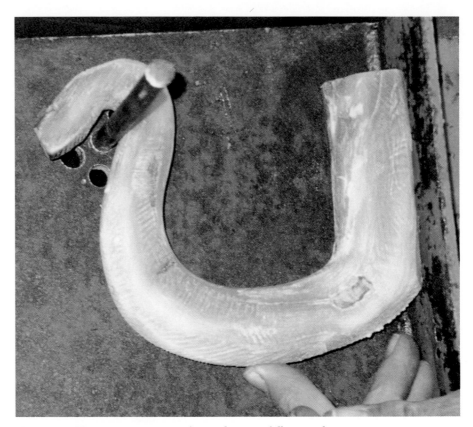

Fig 7.20 *Equipment necessary for producing a fully turned-out nose.*

If, however, you want a more pronounced curl at the nose, as in Fig 7.17, you will not be able to produce it using the above method. You will need some form of fixed peg around which the curl can be shaped, together with a convenient means of securing it when the shaping is complete. The piece of equipment I use for this is shown in Fig 7.20. It comprises a ¼in (6mm) thick steel plate, 13 x 8in (330 x 203mm), to which a 1½in (38mm) deep shoulder of angle iron has been welded across the width at one edge. A cluster of eight ⅜in (10mm) holes has been drilled about 5in (127mm) away from the shoulder and 2½in (64mm) down from the top edge. Another three holes have been drilled at intervals around the perimeter of the plate, about ¾in (19mm) in from the edge. These allow a ⅜in (10mm) bolt to be temporarily inserted as a fixing point to which a G-cramp may be attached to pull the nose round. The bolt can be adjusted from hole to hole in order to maintain pressure on the horn once it starts to move.

Place the part-shaped handle upside down on this plate, with the neck tight up to the shoulder. Then, set the plate in an engineer's vice and

Fig 7.21 *Gently squeezing the heated tip to complete the curl.*

tighten the jaws to secure both the handle and the plate. Introduce a
³⁄₈in (10mm) diameter bolt, about 4in (102mm) long, to one of the
cluster of holes at the point closest to where you want to start the curl in
the nose (*see* Fig 7.20). With the hot air gun, heat a section of horn in
this area, some 3–4in (76–102mm) long, for five minutes or so and, when
ready, bend the horn round the peg until a satisfactory curl is achieved.
Quickly clamp the horn in place on the face of the plate, with G-cramps,
and leave to set. Once set, the horn can be removed from the plate, and
any excess left in the length of the nose can be reduced with a hacksaw.
To complete the curl, clamp the tip in a vice, reheat it, and gently
squeeze it into the required shape (*see* Fig 7.21).

Whatever shape of nose you decide upon, it is important that the tip,
when complete, *looks* complete. Too many crooks I have seen have been
spoiled because the tip has not been finished properly: a half-hearted curl,
an overlong, droopy tip, one cut too short – subjective judgements maybe,
but important nevertheless, particularly when they are made in the
competition tent!

SHANKING THE HANDLE

When you are happy with the shape of the curl you have produced, it's time to shank the handle and bring it to its final finish. You now have three types of shanking joint to choose from:

1 plain
2 with a collar
3 with a spacer

Don't be afraid to use all three (on different sticks of course!) and don't be afraid to experiment: use different materials for the collar and the spacer; try a spacer made from two or three slices of different coloured horn or antler; instead of a plain, straight joint, cut one at an angle. Incidentally, if you *do* cut an angled joint, make it about 45°, with the top of the angle starting at the inside line of the neck and running down the shank (*see* Fig 7.19). The other way round never looks right.

The decision on how to embellish a joint is very much a personal one, but be guided by the quality and colour of the handle and the shank. A coloured buffalo horn handle mounted on an attractive shank, like the example shown in Fig 7.1, needs nothing more to set it off in my opinion, whereas a jet black horn set on a modest shank could benefit from a well-made collar or spacer made from lighter coloured material.

FINISHING

Having shanked the handle, with or without embellishment, proceed to finish its surface with rasps, abrasive paper and cutting polish until all abrasions are removed. Complete the stick by fitting a ferrule and applying a protective finish.

CHAPTER EIGHT

RAM'S HORN CROOKS

W E now come to what most stickmakers would agree to be the most challenging of projects – making a full-size crook from a ram's horn. I have deliberately used the word 'challenging' rather than 'difficult' because if you start with decent material and follow the steps given here patiently, then making a useful crook is *not* difficult. Many of the books I've read make it appear so, with a variety of equipment and complicated techniques, but let's get back to basics. What is certain is that none of this equipment, ingenious though much of it is, would have been available to the first person who made a horn crook and we should never forget that.

CROOKMAKING PROCESSES

It's easy to imagine the first crook being produced by some shepherd who, having picked up a ram's horn, decided to jam it on to the end of his walking staff as a decorative badge of office. From there, the steps towards making it into a working implement are logical and progressive – straightening the curl in the horn, improving the means of attaching handle to shank, and widening the mouth to take a ewe's neck have all resulted in the crook as we know it today.

Crook with hazel shank and one of the best horns I have used from a Welsh mountain ram.

91

The tools and techniques may have changed, but the processes of heat and pressure are still as necessary as they were when, earlier this century, shepherds heated the horn over the naked flame of an oil lamp. This is not a method to be recommended today, although a book on crookmaking which I have, and which was published in 1972, avers that a horn bent by the gentle heat of an oil flame is more likely to keep its shape than that bent using a blow lamp. Of course, stickmakers today would dispute this and be able to point to handles bent by more modern methods which have retained their shape over the years. This is certainly my experience, although I confess I am attracted to the image of a shepherd whiling away long winter nights making crooks by the light of an oil lamp. It conjures up an age when life was less frantic and the passage of time was more leisurely than it is today.

Imagery apart, it is the case that, originally, a minimum number of tools were needed to produce crooks and that is still so. What *has* changed, with the advent of modern equipment, is the length of time needed to make a crook. If you ever reach the stage of making a number of crooks then there can be no argument about the considerable saving in time and effort that the ingenuity of present day techniques produces.

Later in this chapter I will describe some of the equipment which makes my life easier. For now, we will concentrate on building a sequence of basic techniques – many of which have already been introduced – which will result in an acceptable working crook.

PROJECT A

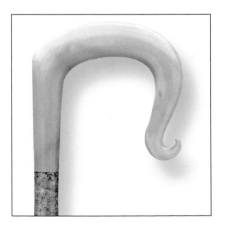

A RAM'S HORN CROOK

Our starting point, as always, is the selection of material, and therein lies our first problem. Use of the word 'selection' implies choice and that is very unlikely to be the case with ram's horn. It is increasingly difficult to come by – particularly in the quality necessary to produce a decent crook. Many of those shown drying out in Fig 8.1 are not up to crookmaking standard. The decision, therefore, is whether to work with what's available or to delay starting until you have acquired something worthwhile. My advice is to make a start with what there is. Whilst your first attempt may not turn out to be the best crook you will ever make, it will provide you with practice, knowledge and experience, all of which will help with your second attempt!

SUITABLE MATERIAL

When you are looking at horn, remember that there are two important factors in determining suitability:

1   the thickness of its wall; and
2   its surface length when measured from base to tip.

Fig 8.1 *A collection of ram's horns.*

Fig 8.2 *Ram's horns vary greatly in their dimensions: compare the base width of these three.*

Ideally, the wall thickness at its base should not be less than ¼in (6mm). Anything much thinner is likely to collapse once we start to squeeze it into shape. As for length, we are going to need a minimum workable length of 16in (406mm). If the horn is already of sufficient thickness at the base, it will not be necessary to cut back the length very much, if at all. On the other hand, if the wall is thin, the length may need to be reduced quite substantially before the wall thickens to a point where it becomes usable. This reduction in length, if it becomes excessive, may leave insufficient material to produce a full-size crook, but, once cut, don't discard it. It may be possible to make a market stick or a Cardigan stick from it. In fact, *never* discard a piece of horn – you will almost certainly find a future use for it. Figure 8.2 shows some examples of horns which, although they are of similar length, vary considerably in thickness at the base. The one on the right, at its thickest, is ½in (13mm) and should produce more than enough material to work with, whilst the one on the left, with a thickness of less than ⅛in (3mm), will need to be cut back considerably before a working thickness is found.

Try to avoid horns which have too much surface damage or too many blemishes – particularly if they occur within the working length you are going to need. If they occur close to the base or tip of the horn, it may be possible to lose them in the making process. Remember, all horns have a concave surface and, at its extreme, this will not be easy to take out, so look for horns where this concavity is not too pronounced.

Even those horns which appear at first to be of pristine quality (and you will not find many of those!) may, as work progresses, develop previously unseen flaws. This cannot be helped. I have made many horn crooks, but I have rarely found the perfect horn: some prove to contain blood blisters (which may have been caused by fighting and which impart a slight reddish hue to the surface), others have small cavities or short splits. As I have remarked before, such faults help to give a natural horn its individual character and in the case of a working crook do not detract from its value.

At this point we are not concerned with the search for perfection though when it comes to stickmaking competitions, that's another question. Instead, let us be guided by the criterion of 'fitness for purpose' and, within the parameters of acceptability I have already described, settle for what's available!

REMOVING THE QUICK

The first step, if it is still contained, is to remove the quick. This can usually be done, you may recall, by giving the base of the horn a few sharp taps against a wooden surface. It should come out readily and in one piece. If it doesn't, and your patience does not extend to letting it dry for another month, try boiling it for half an hour. When cool, a repeat of the tapping process should do the trick. Whatever happens, do not attempt to drill or chisel it out: you will only succeed in damaging the horn or yourself.

When the quick has been removed, it will leave a cavity of corresponding length. This may extend for up to one-third of the length of the horn. The reduction of this cavity by boiling and squeezing the horn is our next step.

BOILING AND BULKING THE NECK

The smell of boiling horn is not particularly pleasant, so whilst the kitchen may be the most obvious place to do it, it is certainly not the best! A portable stove in the workshop is a far better proposition – and I have the luxury of my old water boiler.

Boil the horn for about half an hour and remove it from the container with tongs (*see* Fig 8.3). The section nearest the base, which will form the neck of the crook, now needs to be squeezed or bulked using the same pair of moulds we used to produce the Cardigan stick in Chapter 6. You will recall that these are made from a short piece of 1¼in (32mm) diameter pipe, split in two lengthways. Position the moulds around the horn at its base, then clamp them in the vice and tighten up so that the moulds start to close and force the horn into shape.

Fig 8.3 *Remember a horn will be hot after boiling: use tongs to remove it.*

Fig 8.4 *I insert a steel bolt into the cavity of the horn during bulking to prevent the horn collapsing.*

To prevent the horn collapsing inwards at this stage, I insert a 6in (152mm) steel bolt, of ³⁄₈in (10mm) diameter, into the cavity, as far as it will readily go (*see* Fig 8.4). In order to maintain the horn at a malleable temperature, play a hot air gun along the section contained within the moulds and continue to tighten the vice. You will see that the moulds will probably not be able to close up entirely because, in the squeezing process, a section of horn may have been extruded and this welt will prevent the moulds from closing tightly together. Don't worry about this, and don't try to force the moulds together by excessive pressure in the vice. All this will do is cause the two pieces of the mould to splay outwards.

Leave the horn to cool in the vice overnight and, on removal, use a rasp to take off the extruded sections and generally tidy up what should now be the circumference of the neck section of the handle. The bolt should also be withdrawn from the horn cavity. You will see that the hole it has left is now (almost certainly) off-centre. This does not matter as we shall not be using this hole as a location for the shank. Instead, we shall soon be filling it in and subsequently redrilling another hole centrally, to take the shank.

STRAIGHTENING THE HORN

The next stage is to remove the natural curl in the horn. To do this we need to reheat the horn with the hot air gun and then either sandwich it between two ¹⁄₄in (6mm) thick steel plates, say 9in (229mm) square, under pressure in the vice or clamped with G-cramps, to a single plate. I prefer the latter method as I can see more clearly what's happening to the horn and can quickly adjust the cramps accordingly. I use the steel plate I described in Chapter 7 (illustrated in Fig 7.20). It has the additional advantage of being able to clamp the neck section tightly against the shoulder plate, so preventing it from moving out of alignment with the rest of the horn as the curl is being removed.

Remember when using the hot air gun, not to concentrate heat in any one area for too long – this risks searing or cracking the horn. Play the gun along the 4–5in (102–127mm) section being bent and pull it into line gradually with G-cramps. Once the entire length (excluding the neck) has been heated and clamped into place against the back plate, leave it to cool in the vice.

Whilst it is doing so, use this opportunity to fill the hole in the neck left by the bolt with liquid resin or some equivalent hard-setting liquid.

When the horn is removed from the cramps, it should look like the example shown in Fig 8.5.

BULKING THE CROWN AND NOSE

Bulking requires the use of a series of shaped hard wood or alloy formers which will both squeeze and bend the horn into shape. A set of such formers is illustrated in use in Fig 8.6. They are easily made in wood or can be purchased from the suppliers listed (*see* page 144).

Place them either side of the section of horn to be shaped, and clamp lightly in the vice. Next, heat that section of horn with the hot air gun and tighten the vice until the formers squeeze the surface of the horn into shape.

Fig 8.5 *The desired shape of the horn after bulking and straightening.*

Fig 8.6 *Formers are used, in a vice, to squeeze the horn and bend it into shape.*

Start this squeezing process at the point where the neck of the handle adjoins the crown and continues round to the nose. As we approach this point we should be exerting maximum pressure in order to produce a rounded cross section at the nose which is close to $\frac{1}{2}$in (13mm) in diameter.

Aim to complete this part of the exercise in one go in order to take advantage of the heat which is being retained in the horn. As the formers are gradually moved along it, the horn will assume their shape and its surfaces will become rounded.

Before moving to the next stage in the shaping process, use a rasp to tidy up the surface, removing any high points and rounding over any edges. Take care not to remove too much surplus material.

FINISHING THE NOSE

The section towards the nose now needs to be shaped, using the bending jig, in exactly the same way as we did the buffalo horn crook in Chapter 7 (*see* page 81). Place the horn in the bending jig, use hot air to treat it and G-cramps to pull it round the former. Leave it to set, and on removal it should look like the example shown in Fig 8.7.

Next, decide on the extent of the curl you wish to introduce at the nose, and, having decided, clamp the horn onto the same metal plate we used for the buffalo horn crook in Chapter 7 (*see* page 88). Heat the section you are going to bend, and take it round the pin inserted at that point. Figure 8.8 shows a sash cramp being used to push the horn round the pin and hold it in place until it has set. When it has, any excess length can be carefully trimmed back with a hacksaw.

To round off the curl, the nose can, after heating, be gently squeezed in the vice.

Fig 8.7 *The handle with straightened nose, before the curl is formed.*

Fig 8.8 *Using the sash cramp to curl the nose round the pin.*

One point to note is that the solid section of ram's horn, unlike buffalo horn, contains a central core of white coloured material known as 'flint' or 'gawk'. In a finished handle this can usually be seen when it is held up to the light, and it is also visible when a horn is cut across its diameter. If at all possible, it is desirable to avoid exposing this whiteness, particularly when removing any excess length from the nose. One way of doing so, after the cut has been made, is to use a soldering iron with a broad bit to heat up the very tip of the horn, which may then be teased over to seal off any visible white flint. Whilst this is not a critical operation – especially in the case of your first crook – I mention it so that you have the option of trying it out.

SHANKING THE CROOK

When you have completed the curl at the nose, the handle should be rasped into its final shape before being shanked. Use the template in Fig 8.9 as a guide, but remember that crook handles come in any number of variations. Figure 8.10 shows some of those which you might try in the future.

We shall shank this crook as before with a ³⁄₈in (10mm) diameter metal joining rod (*see* Chapter 6, page 68). When you come to drill the handle, do not be concerned that you will be drilling out much of the resin used earlier to fill in what was the original cavity. The resin that remains will have bonded to the horn and will certainly be strong enough to take and retain the joining rod. Drill the handle and fit the rod.

Having selected your shank – the one I have chosen is a nicely-figured length of hazel – drill it out too, and try the handle for fit. When you are satisfied with the quality of the joint, glue the handle and shank together and leave them to set.

FINISHING THE HANDLE

The surface of the handle now needs to be finished off. Do so using increasingly fine grades of abrasive paper, and remember what I said earlier about the white core of flint. You should try to avoid exposing this core during the sanding process, but because it may have been squeezed off-centre when the handle was bulked, the flint may be closer to one surface than to another. This can make balancing the shape of the handle a difficult task, but, with care, it can usually be achieved. The secret is not to take off too much material from one section without addressing its opposite surface. Even if the flint does come through, don't worry, it will not affect the functional value of the stick. In a show stick it could result in penalties, but, as I've said before, sticks of show quality are not our primary concern.

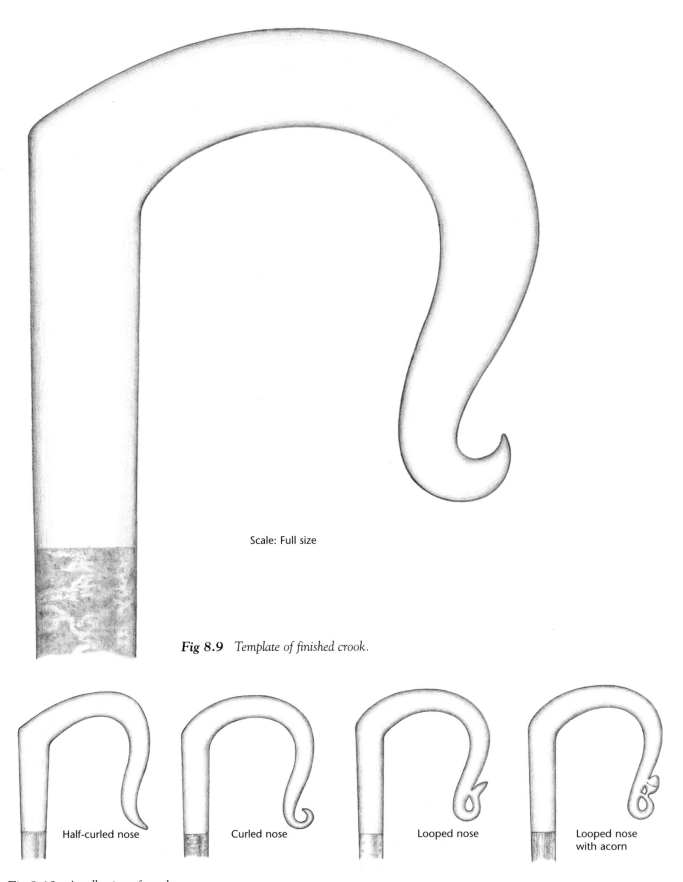

Scale: Full size

Fig 8.9 *Template of finished crook.*

Half-curled nose   Curled nose   Looped nose   Looped nose with acorn

Fig 8.10 *A collection of crooks.*

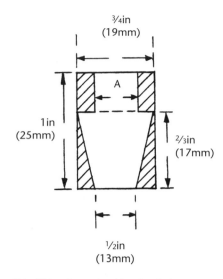

¾in
(19mm)

A

1in
(25mm)

⅔in
(17mm)

½in
(13mm)

'A' will be determined by shank diameter, but will probably be ⅜in (10mm)

Fig 8.11 *Outline and dimensions of ram's horn ferrule.*

FITTING A HORN FERRULE

Polish out any abrasive marks left by sanding, and fit a ferrule. This time, instead of fitting a ready-made ferrule, I'm going to describe how to make one from horn to match the crook handle. Whilst most of the sticks I make are fitted with a metal ferrule, I do think that a well-made ram's horn crook is complemented by a ferrule of the same material. It will be just as durable and is straightforward to make.

Start by selecting an offcut of ram's horn about 1in (25mm) long and of sufficient cross section to accommodate, when finished, the diameter of the shank end. The outline and dimensions of the ferrule we are going to produce are shown in Fig 8.11. Rasp the piece of horn into a cork-like shape and make the dowel at one end with a small hacksaw and file. Drill the shank to take the dowel and adjust for fit until the joint is as good as you can make it. Glue the ferrule in place and leave to set.

Place a turn of masking tape around the shank at the join, to protect the bark, and carefully sand down the circumference of the ferrule until it corresponds with that of the shank. Taper the ferrule slightly and remove the protective tape.

FINISHING

The stick is now ready to finish with a coat of varnish, oil or polish.

SHAPING EQUIPMENT

Earlier in this chapter I mentioned that various pieces of equipment have been developed to facilitate the process of shaping ram's horn, particularly that part which involves bulking the neck or crown under pressure. Many stickmakers have created or developed moulds for this purpose which, with the aid of a car jack in a frame, can be squeezed together under much more pressure than is possible in a vice. I have a set of three such moulds, which can be seen in Fig 8.12. Made from alloy, when the two parts of these moulds are brought together under pressure, they squeeze the horn without allowing any to extrude, as normally happens when simpler, pipe moulds are used.

I find these moulds very useful, but they are relatively costly and such a purchase could only be justified if you intend to produce a number of horn-handled sticks. On the other hand, car jacks, of the hydraulic variety, can often be acquired cheaply from second-hand sources and a simple angle iron frame can be constructed to accommodate one. This combination – even without special moulds – is a useful, and certainly more powerful alternative to using a vice for squeezing operations. As such, a car jack set in a frame is something I would commend as an early 'optional extra'.

Fig 8.12 *Moulds for bulking the neck or crown of ram's horn handles.*

VARIATIONS

If, by this point, you have succeeded in making a crook, what now follows are variations on the main theme. Using a combination of the techniques already described, the production of market sticks (both nose-in and nose-out) and the less common leg crooks, or cleeks, in ram's horn (*see* Fig 8.13) can be tackled without trepidation. From now on, the only governing factor is your own ambition.

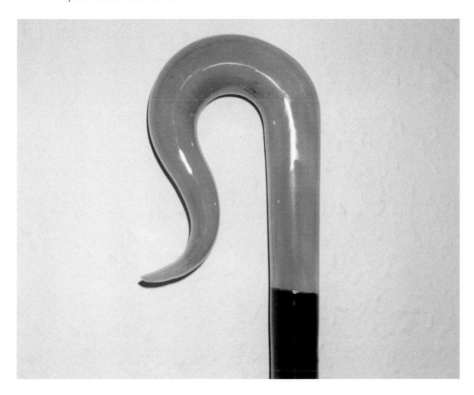

Fig 8.13 *A leg crook, also known as a cleek, in ram's horn.*

1 Draw in outline on flattened nose area

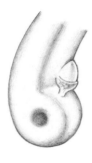

2 Use drill to remove centre of curl and drill small hole near base of acorn stem where it joins the nose

3 Use small rasps to develop shape and contours of acorn

Fig 8.14 *Carving an acorn at the nose of a crook.*

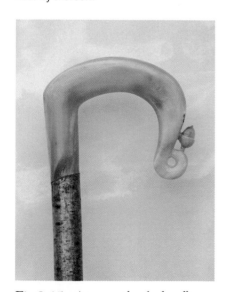

Fig 8.15 *An example of a handle finished with a carved acorn.*

For example, if you want to finish the nose of a crook with something more complicated than a straightforward curl, why not produce a loop (as we did in wood in Chapter 5 – *see* page 55) or carve an acorn or a thistle. The principle in all three cases is the same: instead of bending the horn around a peg to curl it, cut it off at that point, heat it and squeeze the end in a vice until it flattens to a thickness of about ½in (13mm). As it flattens, the surface area will increase, providing the opportunity to introduce the embellishment you have decided upon. Figure 8.14 shows the steps involved in carving an acorn and Fig 8.15 shows the finished product.

Figure 8.16 shows some of the variations I have made. Don't be afraid to experiment – if it all goes wrong, you can always saw off the offending bit and make a smaller handle!

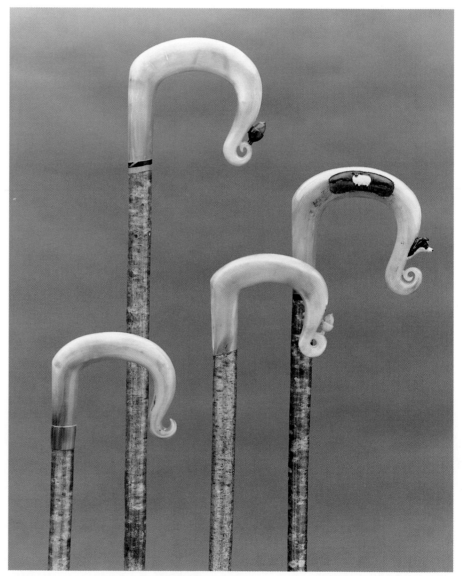

Fig 8.16 *A collection of ram's horn crooks.*

CHAPTER NINE

CARVED STICKS IN WOOD AND HORN

WHILST it is not always the case that good stickmakers make good carvers, it is my experience that once someone has made a crook in wood or horn, it will not be long before he or she wants to try their hand at carving. It is beyond the scope of this book to do other than introduce the topic for, if stickmaking is a craft, then stick carving is an additional art form. We have already touched on the practice in Chapter 3; in this chapter we shall spend a little more time looking at three popular subjects for stick carving:

1 a dog's head (in wood);
2 a pheasant's head (in wood); and
3 a trout (in horn).

It is possible to make any of these in either wood or horn, and I have done so, but the shape and translucence of ram's horn particularly lends itself to the traditional leaping trout. The wooden carvings can be made as one- or two-piece sticks, whilst the trout, in horn, obviously falls into the latter category.

Dog's head market stick carved from lime and joined to shank with horn collar.

ACQUIRING THE WOOD

There are many woods which are suitable for carving, some more exotic and, therefore, more expensive than others. Good timber merchants should have a reasonable variety, but it is likely that you will have to purchase a decent sized block in order to extract the much smaller piece you require. Do not be tempted into paying too much for your first attempt at carving.

It is possible, of course, to obtain wood from other sources. Whenever trees are being felled or branches cut back, there are opportunities to acquire good quality wood in usable quantities at reasonable, if any, cost. The only problem, apart from transportation, is that freshly cut wood has to be properly seasoned before it can be worked and this calls for a degree of patience (*see* page 11)!

Whilst it is perfectly possible to carve handles from most woods, when it comes to finely detailed carvings, like dogs' or birds' heads, many woods are quite unsuitable, particularly for the beginner. Woods to be used for carving need to be clean and close-grained, free of knots and containing no evident flaws – like shakes (splits) – other than surface blemishes. I prefer them to be light in colour if they are to be painted. I have used sycamore, elm, beech and ash to good effect, but one of my personal favourites for carving handles is lime. This is a light-coloured wood with an even grain, which carves easily and is generally available. I recommend it for subjects like animals' and birds' heads.

PROJECT

CARVING A DOG'S HEAD

The dog's head we are going to make here is carved from a suitable block of wood, then shanked in the usual way. Having acquired your block of wood, check it for flaws and irregularities and avoid these, if there are any, when you cut out the piece which you are going to carve.

To produce a dog's head you will need to start with a block of about 4½ x 3½ x 1½in (114 x 89 x 38mm), these dimensions being subject to the breed of dog you wish to reproduce.

The dog chosen as a model for this exercise is a lurcher. Officially a greyhound/collie cross, many mongrels are conveniently, but inaccurately, described as lurchers. This works in our favour because if we don't get the features absolutely right, we can attribute the variations to the pedigree of the model we were using rather than any failings in our skills as carvers! Talking of models, you will see from Fig 9.1 that the one we have chosen is not only photogenic, but a real professional as well.

Fig 9.1 *The perfect model.*

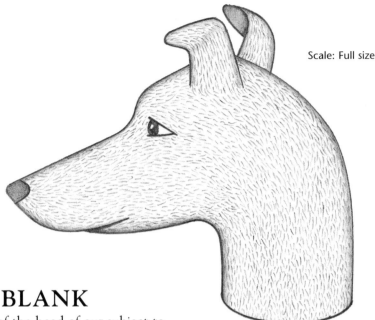

Scale: Full size

Fig 9.2 *Template for head of lurcher.*

CUTTING OUT THE BLANK

Our first step is to produce a line drawing of the head of our subject to the size we want the finished carving to be. Keep it simple since this is only going to be used as a preliminary cutting guide (*see* Fig 9.2). You may find it helpful to make a reference model out of clay or Plasticine so that you can adjust the features – particularly the set of the ears – before you start to carve the wood.

Transfer the drawing you have made to the block of wood using carbon paper, ensuring you have positioned it so that you have an adequate fixing point for the shank in the area of the dog's neck (*see* Fig 9.3). Cut round the outline with a coping saw, bow saw or electric band saw. At first, you may be happier making these cuts in two stages, the first following the outline only approximately to remove most of the waste, and the second following the pencil line more accurately (*see* Fig 9.4). Be careful not to cut into the outline; as always, it is easier to take material off than it is to replace it.

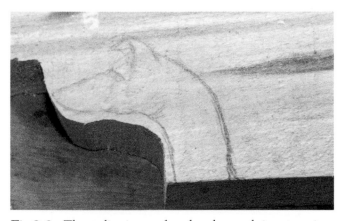

Fig 9.3 *The outline is transferred to the wood, incorporating an area for a workable shank in the neck.*

Fig 9.4 *The outline can be cut out roughly at first before carefully following the lines.*

Having cut out the head, measure and mark a centre line, in pencil, right around the head and neck. This line will help you keep the features in balance and in the correct position on either side of the head as carving progresses.

The next step is to remove waste from both sides of the head. To do so, draw two pencil lines from the nose towards the forehead on the upper surface of the carving to give a realistic plan view. It is critical that these lines are equidistant from the centre line and mirror each other in order to maintain the balance of the head from now on. Set the head at a comfortable angle in the vice and carefully saw along these lines (*see* Fig 9.5). Either side of the neck, take a line from the cheekbone to the bottom of the neck to give a realistic shape and remove these areas of waste as well (*see* Fig 9.6). Use a coping saw to create a gap between the ears for the crown of the head, which should by now be starting to look like that of a dog!

REFINING THE SHAPE

Start to carve by taking off the square edges left by the saw cuts with a sharp knife so that the flat surfaces start to merge into more rounded contours. I generally use a craft knife with a range of replaceable blades which have different shaped cutting edges. To introduce detail, eye sockets, nose, cheekbones, mouth and ears should now be developed, with constant reference to your model (*see* Fig 9.7). From now on it's a question of attempting to replicate nature, but on a smaller scale – no easy task!

Continue the shaping process with a series of small rasps or files until you are satisfied with the conformation and balance of the head, then remove any rasp marks with fine abrasive paper.

Fig 9.5 *Removing the waste from the sides of the head.*

Fig 9.6 *The blank with waste removed from the sides of the neck and head.*

Fig 9.7 *Refer constantly to your model whilst working on the facial details.*

FIXING THE EYES

Now is the time to set the eyes in place. Whilst it is possible to make the eyes yourself, I recommend that you buy them ready-made (the suppliers listed on page 146 have a good range). The size needed will be determined by the animal you are modelling; for this lurcher, I used 3/16in (4mm) eyes. Before gluing them in, try them in the sockets dry, or hold them in place with a small piece of clay or putty. This will provide the opportunity to make any necessary adjustments. It is vital that the eyes are set level with each other and are equidistant from the centre of the nose. If they are not, the finished product will be spoiled.

When you are happy, fix them in place with a small blob of clear, liquid glue, making sure that they are both looking in the same direction – avoid a squint at all costs! (*See* Fig 9.8.)

The head can be painted now or after some additional detail has been scribed in. You can buy scribers (used in metal work to scratch marks in metal), but the arm of a broken compass or even a 2in (51mm) masonry nail ground to a sharp point, and stuck into a cork, are equally effective. A modellers' scalpel is also useful. If you do decide to include further detail, be careful not to overdo it. The surface should not be scratched too deeply or too frequently – to do so risks removing small nicks from the surface and this will spoil the effect you are trying to achieve (*see* Fig 9.9).

PAINTING

To paint the head, start with a coat of sanding sealer – this will provide good adhesion for the subsequent layers of paint. Use whatever medium you are comfortable with to apply the colours; acrylics, oils, watercolours or felt tip pens can all be used effectively. Colour the lightest areas first, and build up the darker colours as you go, finishing with any areas which need highlighting, like the line of the mouth or the inside of the ears.

FINISHING

When you are satisfied with the effect you have produced, set the head aside to dry, then apply two coats of varnish for protection before fixing the shank in the normal way (*see* page 68 and Fig 6.12). Because we have carved this head with the ears in a cocked position, it will not be comfortable to use as a handle for a walking stick. The shank, therefore, needs to be long enough for it to become a market stick which will be held in the area of the dog's neck.

After shanking and fitting a ferrule, two additional coats of varnish should be applied to finish the stick. Figure 9.10 shows the completed stick under the critical eye of the model!

Fig 9.8 *Ensure that the eyes are both facing the same direction when you fix them in position.*

Fig 9.9 *A textured effect resembling dog hair can be created with careful scribing.*

Fig 9.10 *Model and completed stick.*

Fig 9.11 *Heat the horn with a hot air gun . . .*

Fig 9.12 *. . . before bending the ear to shape with pliers.*

MAKING EARS FROM HORN

One of the problems with any kind of carving is that the more detailed it is, the more vulnerable it becomes. This is especially so with sticks intended for practical use as opposed to simply being hung on the wall for display. In this stick, for example, it is evident that the cocked ears, if they are to be realistic, are quite thin and, therefore, susceptible to damage at the point where they bend.

If they are damaged and you need to replace them – or, indeed, if you wish to prevent such a risk in the first place – the ears can be fashioned from a thin slice of horn and glued in position. Whilst some purists might shudder at the thought, I see nothing wrong with such a practice: it will preclude entry in an 'all wood' class at a show, but so what?

If you wish to try this method, or need to effect a repair, cut a flat piece of horn to shape and size, but make it ¼in (6mm) longer than required at the end where it will join the head. Clamp it lightly in a vice, heat with a hot air gun (*see* Fig 9.11) and whilst hot, use long-nosed pliers to bend it into the desired shape (*see* Fig 9.12). Position this ear on the head and mark round the base with a pencil. Cut a ¼in (6mm) deep slot to accommodate the ear, and adjust for fit.

Drill a hole in the base of the ear to take a ¾in (19mm) panel pin, with the head nipped off, then drill a corresponding hole in the slot in the head (*see* Fig 9.13). The pin will act as a reinforcing dowel, adding strength to the ear.

Use epoxy glue to fix the ear in place and fill any visible gaps with plastic filler. When set, sand down the filler and the area where the ears are joined to the head, and the head is ready for colouring (*see* Fig 9.14). On completion, it is difficult to tell that the ear has been added on.

Fig 9.13 *The ears are positioned with a pin 'dowel', which also adds strength to the ear.*

Fig 9.14 *Fix the ear with epoxy glue and sand smooth.*

CARVING A PHEASANT'S HEAD

Pheasants are a popular and traditional subject for the decoration of sticks and can be included in a variety of ways and sizes. I have seen them being chased up the crown of a crook by a fox, being hung lifelessly from the neck of a crook and, perhaps most often, with their head forming the handle for a market stick or walking stick. The one which we are going to make, as a one-piece stick, falls into the last category.

COLLECTING INFORMATION

Before starting work, it is crucial that you acquire a reference model for this head. Not only are there subtleties in a pheasant's head which are rarely identifiable from secondary source material, even from photographs, but the colours and iridescence in the male have to be seen 'in the flesh' to be fully appreciated (*see* Fig 9.15). Few pheasants in the wild will be sufficiently obliging for you to get close enough to admire their plumage, so a visit to your local butcher may be called for. Pheasants are usually in plentiful supply throughout Britain during the autumn months of the shooting season; a brace will not be wildly expensive and they do make a rather splendid meal! For our purposes we need the head with feathers intact, so when you place your order, remember to tell the butcher so that he does not obligingly feather and truss the bird for you beforehand! Get him to remove the head and put it in a polythene bag, then consign it to your freezer until needed. It is the reflection of light in the feathers as a pheasant moves its head that produces the iridescence, so this is obviously lost once the bird is dead, but, if only for the purposes of differentiating colouring, a dead bird is better than none.

It is possible to purchase life-size heads made from synthetic material, and some of these contain a great deal of useful detail (*see* Fig 9.16). Do your homework before you start.

Fig 9.15 *The feathers of the male pheasant have wonderful colours and iridescence.*

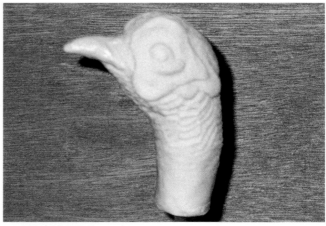

Fig 9.16 *Models of pheasant's heads contain much useful material for carvers.*

SELECTING THE SHANK

The next step is to select an appropriate, seasoned shank complete with block attached. This almost certainly means hazel, but, because the block does not have to be large, it might be possible to find suitable material from sycamore, holly and ash. If you are using hazel, try to find a nicely mottled piece which will complement the shades and colours of the finished head. The length of shank you are looking for will be determined by the type of stick you have decided to make. In this case I settled for a market stick and was able to find a well marked shank which should do justice to the head we are going to produce.

CUTTING OUT THE BLANK

We first need to reduce the size of the block and square it off as we did for the knob stick in Chapter 3 (*see* page 24). Using a panel or electric band saw, cut the block into an approximate cube whose sides are 3in (76mm) long. Transfer the outline of the pheasant in Fig 9.17 to one of the vertical faces of the block, as we did with the dog's head earlier, making sure this time that the neck of the bird is aligned so that it runs into the shank. Carefully remove no more than 1½in (38mm) of bark from the shank where it joins the block so that this area can, in due course, be detailed with feathers.

Cut round the outline with a coping saw or band saw, being careful not to cut into the line. Measure and mark a central pencil line around the head, as with the dog, so that the features will be symmetrical. From this centre line on the upper surface of the head, take a line on either side over to a point close to the top of the beak (*see* Fig 9.18). These guidelines will help you remove the surplus from these areas and start to bring the beak into shape.

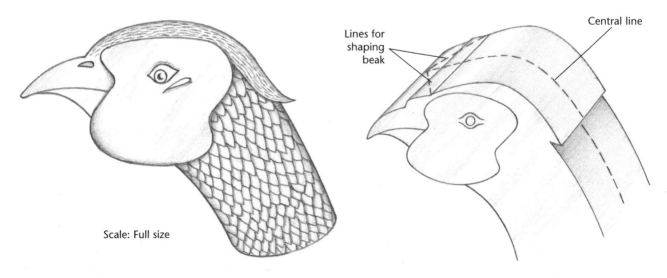

Fig 9.17 *Template for head of pheasant.*

Fig 9.18 *Guidelines for preliminary shaping of head.*

Scale: Full size

Lines for shaping beak

Central line

REFINING THE SHAPE

If you haven't done so already, it is time to retrieve the pheasant from the freezer! From now on you should use it, and any other references you have, as the basis for shaping the head. Unlike the dog's head, where deviations from the model could be attributed to 'breed characteristics', a pheasant which turns out to look more like a buzzard is just not acceptable.

Use a rasp to round over the square edges of the head and remove further surplus in the area of the beak, bringing it to more of a point. The basic head shape should be evident at this stage. Continue to improve the shape of the head until you are satisfied with it.

Some of the finer details should now be pencilled in, notably the position of the eyes and the wattles which surround them. These flaps of skin hang loosely from the cheeks of the bird. The area around them, therefore, needs to be cut back so that the wattles are seen to stand slightly proud of the sides of the head (*see* Fig 9.19). Nick out the sockets for the eyes and, using the same techniques as for the dog's head, position them temporarily before fixing them in place.

Fig 9.19 *The wattles are made to stand proud by cutting back the area around them slightly.*

CREATING TEXTURE

You can now sandpaper the head to remove high spots or imperfections, but do not attempt to produce a perfectly smooth surface finish. What we are looking for is the illusion of feathers and the next step is to create this in and around the neck area.

To achieve the appearance of several rows of overlapping feather tips calls for one of two techniques: either punching them in with a small gouge or burning them in. I have used both to good effect, but find the latter approach an easier one. It does not necessarily require the purchase of expensive pyrography equipment. I use an ordinary electric soldering iron with interchangeable bits, and have simply cut the point off one of these bits and filed the end into a 'U' shape (*see* Fig 9.20). When this is applied to the surface of wood it imprints an acceptable image of a feather tip. Refer to your model and practise on a piece of scrap wood until you achieve the right effect.

Fig 9.20 *To create a feathered effect, I use a cut-off soldering iron to texture the wood.*

When you are confident, imprint descending rows around the neck, starting from the wattles and running towards the shank (*see* Fig 9.21). Any further texturing required on the head can be scratched in with a fine point as for the detail on the dog's head.

PAINTING

The head should now be ready for painting, and in my view it should be painted. I say this because, whilst handles depicting many other species of bird may be left simply varnished, the colours of a pheasant's head cry out to be captured in paint. This is not, however, a simple task, as will be evident when the real thing is examined closely, and if you have not been able to lay your hands on the real thing, you are disadvantaged before you start.

I will not attempt to describe the process of painting here – that is something for you to explore. What I will say is that achieving the iridescent effect is particularly difficult, but it is possible to obtain special paint for this purpose from craft shops or from the supplier listed on page 146.

FINISHING

After painting, finish the stick with a ferrule and give it the usual protective coating.

Fig 9.21   *The feather marks should be imprinted in descending rows down the neck.*

CARVING A LEAPING TROUT

We come now to the third subject in this 'natural history' class, the dream of most fly fishermen – a well-proportioned, leaping trout! Represented as a fish which has just left the water to take a fly, the handle is usually carved from ram's horn in an inverted 'U' shape. I have to say, immediately, that fish do not naturally adopt such contorted attitudes when leaping for flies, but stickmakers have to be allowed some degree of artistic licence if we are to work within the twin constraints of available material and making a practical walking stick.

SUITABLE MATERIAL

Although it is perfectly possible to make a handle like this from wood (*see* Fig 9.22), ram's horn produces a much better effect. It does not require first-rate material; the most important criterion is that it contains sufficient solid material at its tip to allow this area, when squeezed flat, to be shaped into the trout's tail. Figure 9.23 shows the outline we are aiming for.

Select a horn which will provide a minimum of 11in (279mm) of workable material with a wall thickness, after cutting to length, approaching ³⁄₈in (10mm) or more. If necessary, remove the quick and cut the horn to length before boiling for about half an hour.

Fig 9.22 A leaping trout carved from wood.

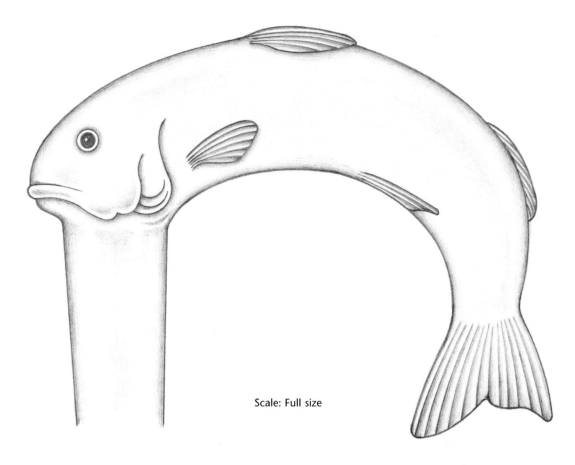

Scale: Full size

Fig 9.23 *Template for leaping trout.*

STRAIGHTENING AND BULKING

On this occasion, we are going to remove the curl in the horn before we start to bulk the neck. When it has boiled for long enough, carefully take it out of the water with tongs and check for pliability. If it moves under pressure, immediately clamp it between 9in (229mm) square metal plates in a vice, or clamp it to a single back plate with three or four G-cramps. Leave it to cool until it sets and then the process of bulking can begin.

Starting with the neck end, heat the horn as we did for the ram's horn crook (*see* page 94), and use the half-round moulds to squeeze the neck and crown sections into shape. For the neck of this stick we only require a length of about 2½in (64mm) below the bottom of the fish's jaws. It should be noted here that the finished cross section of the body will be oval in shape rather than circular. Bear that in mind when bulking up this area.

Continue heating and squeezing to within 1½in (38mm) of the tip – the remaining length of horn will be flattened to produce the tail of the fish.

When you have finished bulking the main area of the body, transfer the heat to the tail section and squeeze it tightly in the jaws of the vice. The object of this is to flatten the section so that it provides a sufficiently large area from which the tail can be shaped.

Now leave the handle to cool. This process may be hastened, if you wish, by spraying it with water. Once cool, the handle is ready for shaping.

ROUGHING OUT THE SHAPE

Begin with the neck of the handle, below the jaw of the fish. Use rasps first, and then abrasive paper, to bring this area to a circular section, tapering slightly upwards from the shank joint to the bottom of the jaw. From this point, the head and the body should assume more of an oval section.

When you have rounded off the neck of the handle, it should be shanked using the metal rod method (*see* page 68). Once you are satisfied with the joint, fix the rod in place in the handle, but not, at this stage, in the shank. The rod, when set, will be a convenient means of holding the handle in position in the vice for carving details and painting.

Before proceeding any further, I suggest you now need to obtain a specimen of a trout so that you can familiarize yourself with its symmetry, shape and colour. No matter how good a photograph may be, it will be no match for seeing the fish in the flesh. Obtaining one presents no problem these days – the freezer cabinet of most supermarkets should oblige.

Although it is unlikely that your handle will be to full scale, the location of the fins, their relationship to one another, the position and size of the eyes, and the shape of the mouth and tail are all important details which can only be obtained from a specimen fish. In addition, when it comes to colouring it, there is no substitute for having a real example in front of you.

Continue to rough out the outline with a fine rasp or file, with reference to your model and to the drawing in Fig 9.23. Remember to leave sufficient high spots on the surface of the body at those points where the fins and gills will be detailed.

REFINING THE SHAPE

Draw in the shape of the tail and cut round it with a coping saw. Decide whether you want to model the fish with its mouth slightly open or closed and shape it accordingly. Most of the trout handles I have seen are made with the tail in line with the head, but it is far more realistic if the body, towards the tail end, is given a bit of a twist sideways so that the tail is out of line and more like it would be in nature. This is easily achieved by using the hot air gun to heat the appropriate area and then, using a cloth to hold it, bending the body to a convincing angle. Help it to set in the chosen position by damping it quickly with cold water.

ADDING EYES

The next step is to introduce the eyes. You can either buy ready-made ones or produce them yourself. To make eyes, drop two or three small blobs of clear glue on to the surface of a piece of stiff, non-absorbent card (a glossy postcard is ideal) and leave them to set. When they have done so, cut out the size of eye required with a sharp knife and carefully flick them off the card. Adjust to fit the eye sockets and position them carefully, before gluing in place. Finish off by colouring the pupil with a very fine paintbrush or felt tip pen.

EXTRA DETAIL

To detail the main features like gills, fins, tail and mouth, use either small chisels and scribers or a pyrograph with a fine bit. Be careful if you elect to use heat, as horn will melt and features may, in consequence, become indistinct. Do not be tempted to overdo the detail of the scales on a trout. I have seen some otherwise excellent examples spoiled because the scales had been made too prominent, making the finished product appear too much like a coarse fish. For your first attempt it may be wiser simply to pick out the main features and make a good job of painting the body, omitting any detailing of the scales. The choice is yours. Whatever you decide, I recommend that you obtain one of the many excellent books on carving and painting fish which are available today. Not only will it inspire you, it will provide a considerable amount of useful information as well. Figure 9.24 shows three stages in the production of a typical trout handle and Fig 9.25 shows an example of a completed stick.

Fig 9.24 *Adding detail: three handles at different stages of production.*

Fig 9.25 *A trout can also be attached to the shank at its tail end.*

CHAPTER TEN

MEDLEY OF STICKS

WHEN I set out to produce this book, it was my intention, by describing within a framework of a limited number of projects, to embrace the broadest possible range of techniques used in the craft of stickmaking. These would culminate, in the final chapter, in the production of a crook made from ram's horn.

Having completed that chapter, I now realize that so many types of stick remain to be described. Several did not readily fall within the project concept of this book and yet they, and probably many others I shall be forced to omit, are worthy of description.

In this chapter, therefore, we shall look at a number of sticks in varying degrees of detail. Some are described only by illustration and caption; they are included to stimulate your ambition by showing what can be achieved with imagination and not a little skill! But let's start with something quite basic.

Thumbstick with lyre-shaped top formed from cow horn.

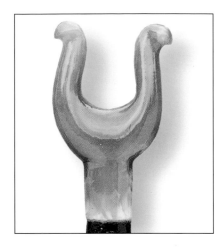

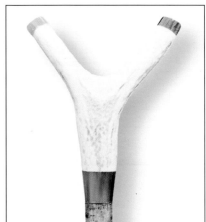

'FANCY' THUMBSTICKS

In Chapter 2, I described how to fashion a natural thumbstick and you will recall that the greatest difficulty this project posed was finding a satisfactory stick which incorporated an acceptable vee. The easiest way of solving that particular problem is to manufacture a separate vee from suitable material and then fit it to a complementary shank.

MATERIALS

The range of suitable materials is considerable – wood, antler, horn, even synthetics like nylon, can all be used to good effect. I have seen a natural 'vee' from one tree grafted on to a shank from another tree of the same species, with the join covered by a collar made from antler. And, of course, antlers themselves often provide attractive vee-shaped tines which require little further shaping to make them acceptable. Those from roe deer are particularly suitable for lightweight sticks, whilst those from red deer can be made into something more robust. For the purpose of scale, the pocket knife in Fig 10.1 has a 2½in (64mm) blade.

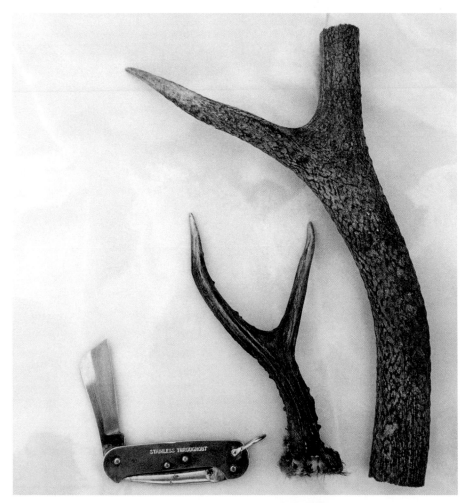

Fig 10.1 *Potential thumbsticks. Left: roe deer. Right: red deer.*

FITTING CAPS

In both cases, when the sides of the vee have been cut to length, the porous core of the antler will have been exposed. A cap will, therefore, need to be fitted to the top of both sides in order to finish them off. Such caps are usually cut from a piece of contrasting material – black buffalo horn is attractive – and are shaped close to finished size before being glued in place. To strengthen the joint it is good practice to drill a few small holes in the underside of the cap and the top of the antler tine to allow the glue to penetrate both surfaces and provide improved adhesion (*see* Fig 10.2). Take care not to drill right through the cap as this will spoil its surface. Use epoxy glue to fit the caps in place and, when set, use abrasive paper to finish them off.

If the neck of the antler handle is inclined to be oval at its base, do not simply file it round to make it fit the shank. Instead, fit a spacer which will allow you to adjust the circumference of both of its ends to correspond with that of the handle and the shank (*see* Fig 10.3).

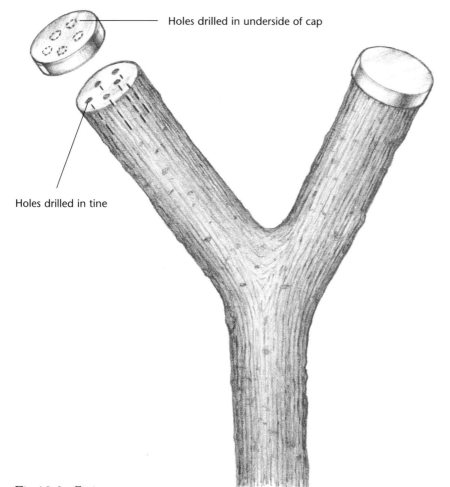

Holes drilled in underside of cap

Holes drilled in tine

Fig 10.2 Fitting a cap.

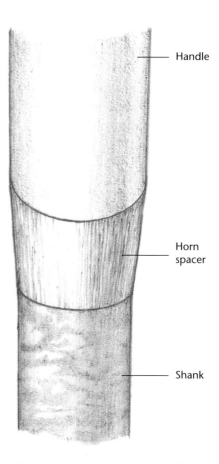

Handle

Horn spacer

Shank

Fig 10.3 A spacer can be used to match an oval handle base with a circular shank top.

ADDITIONAL CARVING

As an alternative to a simple cap to finish off the tines, it is possible to carve the small head of a suitable subject and fit that instead. Sporting dogs are popular and Fig 10.4 shows what can be achieved using a three-tined antler and a trio of terriers. Figure 10.5 is a working stick in more than one sense. Whilst the ubiquitous collie appears on one of the tines, the other has been converted into a whistle. This is a straightforward process and makes a useful 'extra'. Figure 10.6 shows the steps involved.

Fig 10.4 *For a more elaborate stick, carved heads can be fitted in place of caps.*

Fig 10.5 *A functioning whistle has been carved from this antler tine.*

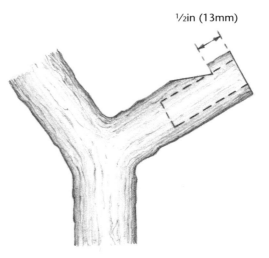

½in (13mm)

1 Cut the tip of the tine off squarely and drill a central hole in the remaining wood, about 1½in (38mm) deep and ⅜in (10mm) in diameter.

2 Cut a notch about ½in (13mm) from the end so that it just penetrates the hole.

3 Tidy up the notch with a sharp knife or chisel.

4 Cut a 1½in (39mm) length of ⅜in (10mm) diameter dowel and shave off almost half the diameter to create a flat surface along its length.

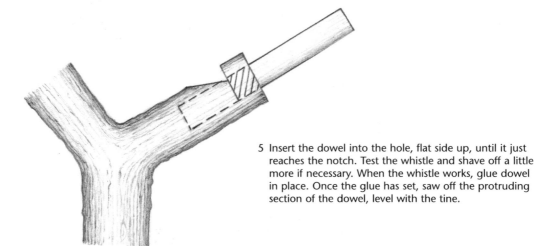

5 Insert the dowel into the hole, flat side up, until it just reaches the notch. Test the whistle and shave off a little more if necessary. When the whistle works, glue dowel in place. Once the glue has set, saw off the protruding section of the dowel, level with the tine.

Fig 10.6 *Carving a whistle from an antler tine.*

It's also possible to carve the entire thumbstick piece, dogs and all, from a single block of wood. The advantage of this is that you start from scratch, without being bound by any of the restrictions which, say, the natural contours of an antler present. Figure 10.7 shows a part-carved thumbstick of this type depicting a brace of retrievers. When it is finished it will be mounted, with a horn collar, to a nicely coloured hazel shank. Figure 10.8 shows a variation on the same theme: a short-tailed pointer leaping a ditch.

Fig 10.7 *This thumbstick has been carved from a single block of wood.*

Fig 10.8 *Because it removes the restrictions imposed by a natural thumbstick, carving from a single block gives greater design freedom.*

Of course, carving like this does call for a degree of skill and patience, but it is not as difficult as it might at first appear. If you want to start with something simpler, why not design your own thumbpiece and transfer that to an attractive piece of wood? Figure 10.9 shows one I have made, using a burr from a silver birch. It is an especially comfortable design, details of which are provided in Fig 10.10. Cut out the blank with a coping saw and, with a series of rasps and abrasive paper, bring it to shape.

Fig 10.9 *An attractively grained wood can be very effective in a simple design.*

Fig 10.10 *Template for thumbstick shown in Fig 10.9.*

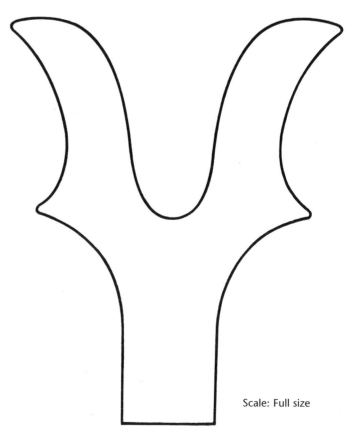

Scale: Full size

USING HORN

Similar principles can be applied to producing thumbpieces from horn. The greatest problem here is to find a horn of sufficient size to provide adequate workable material – less difficult in the case of buffalo horn than ram's horn. This is where some of the big horns come into their own, offering, as they do, enough material to make more than one stick.

To make a horn thumbpiece like that shown in Fig 10.11, you will need a flat, rectangular section of buffalo horn, 3½ x 3 x 1in (89 x 76 x 25mm). Using a paper template taken from Fig 10.12, stick it in place as a cutting guide on one surface of the horn, which has previously been filed clean. Cut out the shape with a coping saw, round off with rasps and finish with abrasive paper and polish. Shank, using a metal rod, with or without a spacer. The only limitation to designing thumbpieces like those described is your own imagination, so go ahead and use it!

Fig 10.11 *A simple thumbstick with a handle of black buffalo horn.*

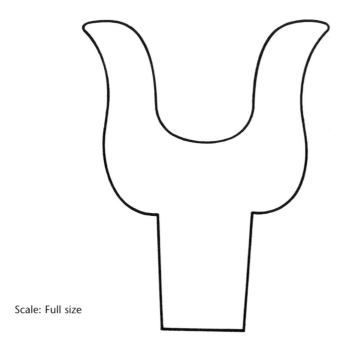

Scale: Full size

Fig 10.12 *Template for thumbstick shown in Fig 10.11.*

HALF-HEAD HANDLES

A design which falls somewhere between that of a crook and a Cardigan walking stick is probably the best way to describe what are called half-head handles. Usually made either as one-piece wooden sticks or from buffalo horn or ram's horn, and in most cases to the length of a market stick, they are comfortable in use as well as being decorative. Such sticks lend themselves to having the head of an animal or a bird carved at the tip of the handle. Popular subjects include badgers, foxes, otters, foxhounds, horses, pheasants and ducks.

SUITABLE SHANKS

If a stick is to be made from one piece of wood, it is important to select a shank which has a good block coming off it at the correct angle. This must be capable of providing a workable area of wood, when measured across the crown from neck to tip, of about 9in (229mm). To some extent, this length can be varied to accommodate the subject chosen: for example, pheasants, ducks, badgers and otters do not present the problem of protruding ears that dogs and horses do, so these heads can be carved closer in to the crown of the stick than the others without affecting its comfortable use. Dogs and horses, if their ears are to be included realistically, may have to be carved further away from the crown to avoid any protrusion resulting in the handle being uncomfortable to grip. Figures 10.13, 10.14 and 10.15 illustrate this point.

PROJECT

125

Scale: Full size

Fig 10.13 *Comparison of handle length required for fashioning different animal heads.*

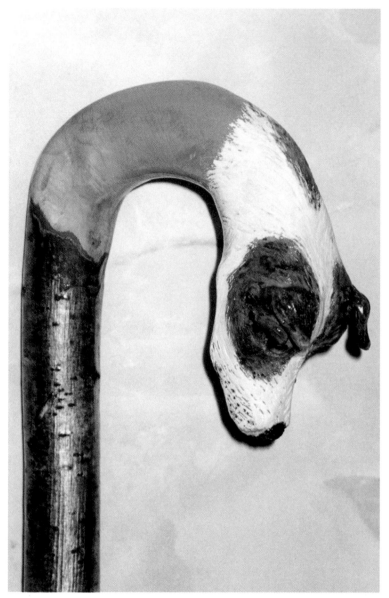

Fig 10.14 *Compare the length of handle required to accommodate the ears of this dog's head . . .*

Fig 10.15 *. . . with the length required for this smooth snake's head.*

SHAPING A HANDLE IN WOOD

Having selected a shank with a suitable block, square off the block as we have done previously and transfer a drawing of your chosen subject on to it, ensuring that the handle flows nicely into the shank. Cut round the drawing carefully and bring the crown and neck areas into a round cross section before starting to shape the head of the subject. Use a coping saw to cut out the profile and then small rasps, a craft knife and possibly a small gouge to develop the contours of the head. If you make a mistake with the ears or beak in doing so, this is easily remedied by fashioning a replacement out of horn and fixing it in place with epoxy glue.

FINISHING

Sand down the handle, paint the head and finish the stick with a ferrule and protective varnish. Figures 10.14 and 10.15 show what can be achieved in both one- and two-piece wooden sticks.

SHAPING A HANDLE IN HORN

To make a half-head out of horn, your first decision is whether to use ram's horn or buffalo horn. Both can be used to equal effect and it may be that the predominant colour of your subject will determine your choice of horn.

You will need a horn with a workable section of about 9in (229mm) and, in the case of ram's horn, any hollow section will need to be squeezed up so that you are working with as much solid material as can be produced. You may find it beneficial to shank the handle from the tip end as we did with the Cardigan stick in Chapter 6: the determining factor will be which end of the horn offers the most promising section for carving.

When you have made your decision, cut the horn to the length you intend to use and roughly trim it to section with a rasp. Boil it for half an hour and, using the pipe moulds, squeeze the neck into shape as necessary.

With the neck in the vice, heat the point at which you intend to bend it with a hot air gun, pull it round a former and clamp it in place to cool and set. Then, rasp and sand the neck and crown, up to the intended carving, into a round cross section of the same diameter as the shank. Draw in the outline of the head, cut round the profile, and shape to finish with small rasps and abrasive paper.

A COW HORN HANDLE

Until now, little mention has been made of the properties and uses of cow horn. That is because it is particularly difficult to obtain these days in the size and quality needed to make the handle of a crook like those shown in Fig 10.17. Like ram's horn, when the quick is removed it is hollow for a good portion of its length, and if the wall of the horn is thin it is difficult to squeeze up successfully.

Nevertheless, it is possible to acquire the occasional horn and if it turns out to be too thin to make into a crook or even a market stick, don't reject it – make an attractive walking stick handle from it.

Fig 10.16 *Cow horn cut to size to produce the handle.*

CUTTING AND CLEANING

Saw off the tip end at a point which will produce a minimum diameter of 1in (25mm). This is the end which will be used to join the handle to the shank, so the diameter should be slightly larger than the shank you have selected. From this cut, measure and mark 3in (76mm) and cut round the circumference at that point. Be careful with this cut; keep it square but angle it slightly. You are now left with a hollow, slightly tapering, 3in (76mm) tube of horn (*see* Fig 10.16).

Clean the external surface using diminishing grades of abrasive paper until you have removed all roughness and any blemishes. Check that the cut ends are square, and correct if necessary.

Fig 10.17 *Cow horn of the quality used in these crooks is rare.*

FILLING THE HOLLOW

Cut a 3in (76mm) length of ¼in (6mm) engineers' studding and insert 1½in (38mm) of this into the narrower end of the horn. With any luck the horn at this point will be solid; drill into and through it to the horn cavity. Centre the rod so that it is vertical and hold it in place with a small internal plug of putty or Plasticine (*see* Fig 10.18). This plug will help to prevent seepage of the liquid resin which is about to be introduced. Set the horn in a vice, making sure that the top is level, and tighten the jaws to grip the studding. Pour in liquid resin, of the kind used to make domed paperweights, until it reaches the rim, but be very careful not to overfill – resin overflowing is a very sticky problem indeed! Leave to set.

When it has done so, paint the surface of the resin (being careful not to smudge the rim of the horn), with a matt neutral colour which will provide a suitable backcloth for the object which is about to be displayed

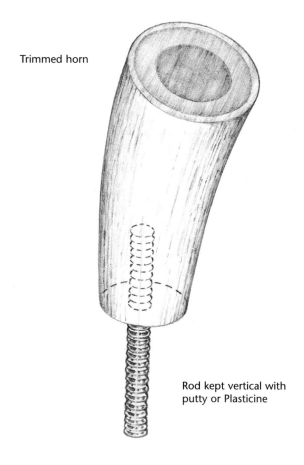

Trimmed horn

Rod kept vertical with
putty or Plasticine

Fig 10.18 *Positioning the joining rod centrally in the horn.*

against it. Wrap two turns of masking tape around the circumference at this end, allowing the tape to extend about ½in (13mm) beyond the rim, thus forming a temporary collar. This will act as a reservoir to contain the next lot of liquid resin (*see* Fig 10.19). Avoid the tape wrinkling inwards as this will affect the surface of the resin when it sets.

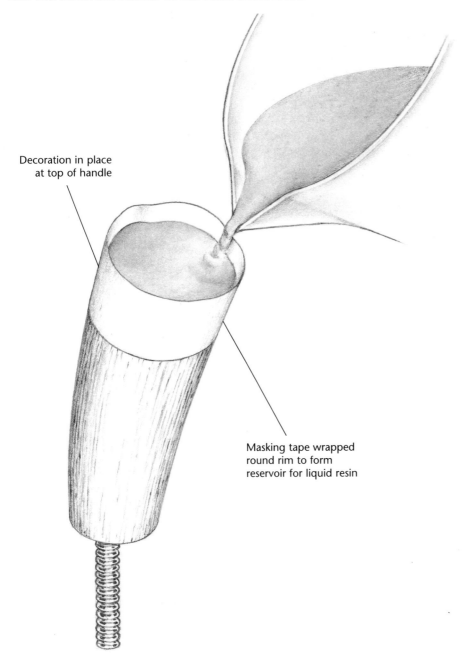

Decoration in place at top of handle

Masking tape wrapped round rim to form reservoir for liquid resin

Fig 10.19 *Sealing the decoration with resin.*

ADDING THE DECORATION

Select an ornamental centrepiece which can be set into the top of the handle – a coin, badge, small brooch or fishing fly can all look good, but remember to remove any clasps from jewellery, and be sure that the item will sit flat on the surface. If it wobbles when it is put in place, use a touch of quick-setting glue to hold it centrally. For this project I used a farthing coin which I polished to a bright finish with metal polish.

When in position, slowly pour in clear resin until the item is completely covered, again avoiding any overflow. Be especially careful to prevent bubbles appearing in the resin: if these are allowed to set they will spoil the effect. Should any appear, slide them gently to the edges with a needle so that they can be sanded out in the final process. Leave the resin to set (for at least 24 hours) until it is perfectly hard, then remove the masking tape collar. To ensure that it has properly cured, leave it for another 24 hours before starting work on it.

FORMING THE DOME

What now remains is to shape the resin top into a symmetrical dome so that it becomes a miniature display case for the ornament contained within.

Use a good file to start with, and don't be concerned that your first file stroke appears to have permanently spoiled the transparency of the surface. Take heart! The white abrasions produced by the file will come out in due course! Continue filing until you are satisfied with the symmetry of the dome.

With increasingly fine grades of abrasive paper, complete the shaping process. You will see that, as the file marks disappear, the transparency of the dome is restored.

Examine the surface in daylight to check that all abrasions have been removed and improve the finish by rubbing it with steel wool which has been dipped in metal polish.

Finally, use metal polish on a cloth to produce a blemish-free dome.

FINISHING

Fix the handle to the shank, fit a ferrule and apply a protective finish to complete the stick.

A BARLEY TWIST NOVELTY

For our final stick, I have chosen one which I think will appeal to those who are attracted to making a stick with mathematical precision! The only problem is that this stick, if properly produced, will give the impression to most observers that it has been machine made. Convincing them that you have made it using the most basic of hand tools should be fun.

CUTTING AND MARKING

To start, you need a 36in (914mm) length of 1in (25mm) dowel rod which is straight, close-grained and unflawed. Such material is readily available in most shops in the form of a broom handle.

Having cut the rod to length, divide the circumference at one of its ends into thirds. From each of the three points on the circumference, draw a parallel line along the entire length of the rod and then divide each of these three lines into 12 sections of 3in (76mm) each.

Starting at the top of the rod, draw a diagonal to link one line with the next at the first 3in (76mm) intersection. Repeat this process with the remaining lines and continue to link the corresponding intersections with diagonals so that a series of three spiral lines is eventually drawn along the whole length of the rod (see Fig 10.20). To draw these spirals accurately takes a little time and patience, but it is important that you get this part of the exercise right. You will find it helpful to use a piece of flexible material as a straight edge to draw the lines or, alternatively, wrap masking or insulating tape around the length of the rod in order to line up the diagonals with the 3in (76mm) intersections.

When you have finished drawing in the spirals, check that they look right – it is all too easy to make a mistake at this stage.

Link the 3in (76mm) sections with diagonal lines

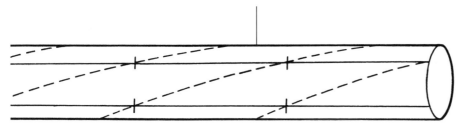

Fig 10.20 *Marking on the guidelines for creating spirals.*

CREATING SPIRALS

If they *are* symmetrical, take a ¼in (6mm) round rasp and, starting 1in (25mm) from the top, carefully follow the first spiral, filing the continuous line to a depth of about ¼in (6mm). Continue with the first line for 6in (152mm) before moving on to the second and then the third lines, in each case proceeding no further than about 6in (152mm) down the length of the rod. Working on all three spirals for a short length at a time will enable you to see how your work is progressing and will help to keep the spirals in proportion to one another. When you have completed the first 6in (152mm) section, the barley twist effect should be apparent (*see* Fig 10.21). Continue to open up the lines in 6in (152mm) sections until you have worked along the complete length of the rod.

Use medium to fine abrasive paper (emery cloth is ideal), wrapped round a piece of suitable dowel, to clean and round out the grooves created by the rasp; this will improve their appearance. Now, give the entire length a light sanding to enhance the barley twist effect.

Fig 10.21 *The barley twist effect.*

FINISHING

This flamboyant shank needs to be complemented with an equally striking handle. It could take a perfectly round wooden one, an antique chased metal one or, as in this particular case, a handsome piece of antler which has had a dog's head carved at the neck end of the tine in a similar way to the stick described in Chapter 6 (*see* page 72). Whatever you decide, the stick should be shanked in the usual way, varnished for protection and fitted with a ferrule to finish it off.

VARIATIONS

The shank of this stick is not unlike that of the antique example shown in Fig 10.22, which has a symmetrically knobbled shank topped with a carved hand holding a snake. As you can see, the handle has been badly affected by woodworm – the stick was brought to me for repair. I am not sure how the shank has been figured in this way, but it is certainly a conversation piece.

Fig 10.22 *Another geometric approach – symmetric knobbles.*

GALLERY

To me, one of the great joys of stickmaking is to admire fine examples of the work of other stickmakers. Not only are they a joy to see, they also provide me with lots of ideas for future projects. With this in mind, the following selection of sticks is intended to show what can be achieved with patience, persistence and practice.

An exquisitely carved kingfisher by Steve Kime whose studies from nature also appear on pages 136 and 137.

A birdwatcher's treat. From left: hummingbird, golden eagle and green woodpecker. (All sticks by Steve Kime.)

The common and the not-so-common: sparrow, snipe and badger. (All sticks by Steve Kime.)

This market stick, with a sheep dog carved into the beech handle, is by Glyn Gillard, winner of the Champion Stickmaker's Shield at the Welsh Game Fair in 1996.

A variation on the sheep dog theme, this time in horn, by Brian Thomas, who is renowned for his skill in producing life-like trout such as that shown on page 116.

If you don't like snakes, I guarantee you would not dare pick up this market stick by Glyn Gillard.

A collection of wooden crooks by Andrew Jones. The two on the left have hazel shanks topped with hardwood handles; the one on the right is carved from a single hazel block.

Black horn crooks by Andrew Jones. The top two are buffalo and the botom one, carved to represent a black-faced mountain ram, is from that type of sheep.

This close-up shows the intricacy of Andrew's ram's head carving.

SUPPLIERS

WOOD, HORN AND STICKMAKING COMPONENTS

Dafydd W. Davies
Y Ddol
Llandewi Brefi
Ceredigion SY25 6RS
Tel: 01974 298566
Wide range of stickmaking components and equipment. Horn and antler, wooden handle blanks, banding jigs and moulds. Crooks made to commission.

Planks and Blanks
24 Bamburgh Road
Newton Hall
Durham DH1 5NW
Tel: 01913 868964
Hardwood handle blanks cut to your own design or 'off the shelf'.

Hillend Horncraft
85 Hillend Road
Clarkston
Glasgow G76 7XT
Tel: 0141 6395735
Suppliers of buffalo horn and antler, pre-formed horn handles and completed sticks and sundries. Demonstrations of bending techniques arranged.

Richard Llewellyn Evans
Rhos Eirin
Maenclochog
Clunderwen
Pembrokeshire SA66 7LD
Tel: 01437 532716
Stickmaking materials including selected shanks with or without blocks, ram's horn, ferrules, joining rod and sundries.

Stroud Metal Co. Ltd
Dudbridge
Stroud
Gloucestershire GL5 3EZ
Tel: 01453 763331
Manufacturers of a wide range of ferrules (including mountaineering spikes) and metal collars.

Tiverton Sawmills
Blundells Road
Tiverton
Devon EX16 4DE
Tel: 01884 253102
Suppliers of a variety of woods (including burrs) suitable for carving into handles. Available by mail order internationally.

TOOLS AND EQUIPMENT

Peter Child
The Old Hyde
Little Yeldham
Halstead
Essex CO9 4QT
Tel: 01787 237291
Manufacturers of pyrography equipment and materials.

John Boddy's Fine Wood & Tool Store Ltd
Riverside Sawmills
Boroughbridge
North Yorkshire YO5 9LJ
Tel: 01423 322370
Extensive range of wood, abrasives, finishes, carving tools, knives and files. Woodcarving courses.

Robert Sorby
Athol Road
Sheffield S8 0PA
Tel: 0114 255 4231
Makers of fine hand tools including micro woodcarving chisels and gouges, and a range of knives.

Pintail Carving
80 Sheppenhall Grove
Aston
Nantwich
Cheshire CW5 8DF
Tel: 0270 780056
Mail order suppliers of carving tools and equipment, books and materials for carving birds and fish, including model heads, glass eyes and specialist paints.

Bristol Design (Tools) Ltd
14 Perry Road
Bristol BS1 5BG
Tel: 0117 929 1740
Suppliers of woodworking hand tools including micro carving knives, chisels and gouges.

PAINTS AND FINISHES

Fred Aldous
PO Box 135
37 Lever St
Manchester M60 1UX
Tel: 0161 236 2477
Suppliers of craft materials by mail order, including paints, knives, clear embedding resin and hardener.

GLASS EYES

Snowdonia Taxidermy Studios
Llanrwst
North Wales LL26 0HU
Tel: 01492 640664
Range of glass eyes for animals, birds and fish. Available by mail order internationally.

METRIC CONVERSION TABLE

INCHES TO MILLIMETRES AND CENTIMETRES

MM = MILLIMETRES   CM = CENTIMETRES

INCHES	MM	CM	INCHES	CM	INCHES	CM
1/8	3	0.3	9	22.9	30	76.2
1/4	6	0.6	10	25.4	31	78.7
3/8	10	1.0	11	27.9	32	81.3
1/2	13	1.3	12	30.5	33	83.8
5/8	16	1.6	13	33.0	34	86.4
3/4	19	1.9	14	35.6	35	88.9
7/8	22	2.2	15	38.1	36	91.4
1	25	2.5	16	40.6	37	94.0
1 1/4	32	3.2	17	43.2	38	96.5
1 1/2	38	3.8	18	45.7	39	99.1
1 3/4	44	4.4	19	48.3	40	101.6
2	51	5.1	20	50.8	41	104.1
2 1/2	64	6.4	21	53.3	42	106.7
3	76	7.6	22	55.9	43	109.2
3 1/2	89	8.9	23	58.4	44	111.8
4	102	10.2	24	61.0	45	114.3
4 1/2	114	11.4	25	63.5	46	116.8
5	127	12.7	26	66.0	47	119.4
6	152	15.2	27	68.6	48	121.9
7	178	17.8	28	71.1	49	124.5
8	203	20.3	29	73.7	50	127.0

INDEX

ABOUT THE AUTHORS

ANDREW JONES

Born into a farming family, Andrew has spent the whole of his working life farming in west Wales. An uncle cultivated his interest in making sticks and encouraged him to enter his work in local craft shows. He makes a wide range of sticks, but it is his specialities – horn crooks and Cardigan walking sticks – which regularly earn him top honours at major competitions throughout Wales.

He and his wife now live near Lampeter.

CLIVE GEORGE

After a career in the Civil Service, Clive took early retirement in 1993 and, having bought a smallholding, went on to buy a few sheep to go with it. He now owns a small flock of purebred Llanwenog sheep (named after the west Wales parish where he and his wife live) which he shows successfully in his locality.

A life-long interest in stickmaking, and a fortuitous meeting, led him to collaborate in the production of this book.

Andrew (left) is holding a one-piece crook made from hazel. Clive's crook has a golden hazel shank topped with black buffalo horn. They are accompanied by a champion Llanwenog ram and Clive's retired collie 'Jed'.